A Primer for Pastors

A Primer for Pastors

a handbook for strengthening ministry skills

Austin B. Tucker

A Primer for Pastors: A Handbook for Strengthening Ministry Skills
© 2004 by Austin B. Tucker

Published by Kregel Publications, a division of Kregel, Inc., P.O. Box 2607, Grand Rapids, MI 49501.

All rights reserved. No part of this book may be reproduced, stored in a retrieval system, or transmitted in any form or by any means—electronic, mechanical, photocopy, recording, or otherwise—without written permission of the publisher, except for brief quotations in printed reviews.

Unless otherwise noted, Scripture quotations are from the *Holy Bible, New International Version®*. NIV © 1973, 1978, 1984 by International Bible Society. Used by permission of Zondervan Publishing House. All rights reserved.

Scripture quotations marked KJV are from the *King James Version* of the Holy Bible.

Scripture quotations marked NASB are from the *New American Standard Bible*. © The Lockman Foundation 1960, 1962, 1963, 1968, 1971, 1972, 1973, 1975, 1977, 1995.

Scripture quotations marked TEV are from *Today's English Version*. Copyright © 1976 by the American Bible Society.

Scripture quotations marked NEB are from *The New English Bible: New Testament*. Copyright © 1961 by Oxford and Cambridge University Press.

The Williams version is by Charles B. Williams, *The New Testament in the Language of the People*.

Cover design: John M. Lucas

Library of Congress Cataloging-in-Publication Data
Tucker, Austin B.
   A primer for pastors: a handbook for strengthening ministry skills / by Austin B. Tucker.
     p. cm.
Includes bibliographical references.
   1. Pastoral theology. 2. Clergy—Office. I. Title.
BV4011.3.T88   2004
253—dc22   2004001347

ISBN 0-8254-3886-1

Printed in the United States of America
04 05 06 07 08 / 5 4 3 2 1

*To Beverly,
who should write the book
for the pastor's wife.*

Contents

Acknowledgments 9
Introduction: A Noble Task 11

1. Your First Pastorate 17
2. The Pastor Among His People 31
3. Pastoral Care and Counseling 43
4. The Pastor's Pulpit Ministry 53
5. Problem-Solving Preaching 71
6. Pastoral Leadership 83
7. Conflict Management 94
8. Weddings and Funerals 106
9. Ministerial Ethics 120
10. The Bivocational Pastor 130
11. The Pastor as Teacher 141
12. The Pastor as Evangelist 153
13. Baptism and the Lord's Supper 165
14. The Pastor's Stewardship of Time 179
15. The Pastor's Personal Life 202

Notes 212
Select Bibliography 219

ACKNOWLEDGMENTS

THIS BOOK PRESUMES TO OFFER GUIDANCE to those who are beginning a life of pastoral ministry. Some who have known me as pastor might think it peculiarly presumptuous. Let me admit from the start that I do not claim to be the expert on all things pastoral. What I do bring to the task is a providential melding of practical experience and academic training with a strong desire to be helpful. I thank God for the contribution of every teacher and every book that helped shape my understanding. Still, nothing can replace the lessons learned in the laboratory of life.

Among those to whom I owe a great debt are my first pastor and church, T. C. Pennell and Ingleside Baptist Church, Shreveport, Louisiana. I did not know how rich that godly heritage was until I had moved on from his shepherding care to become a pastor. The churches and schools in Louisiana, Texas, and Virginia where I taught others, at the same time taught me.

Recently, I read again a prize-winning book by David M. Dawson Jr., *More Power to the Preacher*.[1] My Aunt Yvonne gave me that little volume over forty years ago when, as a teenager, I first answered God's call to ministry. It reminded me how much a book can shape and inform one who is ready to learn. Since then, other books have made contributions, and in the pages that follow I try to give credit where I know it is due.

I am grateful that Wayne McDill urged Jim Weaver of Kregel Publications to seek me out. Jim did so and invited me to submit a proposal. Then he guided it through the editorial committee and the whole book-building process. Additional thanks to Steve Barclift and the editorial staff at Kregel, who offered hundreds of helpful refinements, and to Wendy Widder for her help with publicity.

I wish to thank friends, young and old, who agreed to read some of these chapters and offer advice: L. Ray Branton, Jason Foster, Wayne McDill, Harold McNabb, and Tommy McKinnon. Also, my long-suffering wife, Beverly, who read every line. They deserve much credit for strengthening this work, but don't blame them for any weakness that filters through.

introduction

A NOBLE TASK

DAVID FISHER ONCE TOLD of a pastor friend who—with two years left before retirement—was having thoughts of continuing to work beyond age sixty-five. It was hard for him to think of leaving the congregation he had served for twenty-eight years. He decided, however, in favor of retirement. "It's too intense," he said, adding that most of the time he felt like a Winnie the Pooh teddy bear being dragged down the stairs, its head banging on every step.[1]

Many experienced pastors will identify with his ambivalence as well as his analogy. The work of the pastor is wonderful work—if you can stand it! "If anyone sets his heart on being an overseer," said Paul to Timothy, "he desires a noble task" (1 Tim. 3:1). If you are just starting this vocation, take courage! A pastor's work is a tremendous task, and it is honorable and good work. None other than the ascended Christ Himself gives to His churches those who will be her pastors and teachers. It is God's plan from eternity that through this ministry the whole body of believers may be more and more conformed to the perfection found only in Christ (see Eph. 4:11–13). What a calling! What an undertaking!

Someone will wonder if it is not a little self-serving to seek a position of such nobility. The nobility is not so much in the office of overseer as in the honorable work done by this shepherd of souls. Still, is it right to set one's heart on this noble task? First Timothy 3:1 in *The New English Bible* says that "to aspire to leadership is an honorable ambition." When does this aspiration, however, become selfish ambition? Jeremiah's message to Baruch is good counsel for any pastor: "Should you then seek great things for yourself? Seek them not" (Jer. 45:5). One should not aspire to a position of greatness as James and John did when, through their mother, they petitioned for the privilege to sit on thrones as vice-regents in Christ's kingdom. It is not easy to distinguish between commendable aspiration and selfish ambition, but it is an important distinction.

Most of us in the evangelical ministry think that we are placed in this task by divine appointment. God called us to do the work of a pastor. It is not just another occupation that one may select. The truth is that it is both a divine choice and a human choice. God arrested Moses in the wilderness by the strange sight of a bush that burned but did not burn up. God called Moses in a voice from that burning bush, "So now, go. I am sending you to Pharaoh to bring my people the Israelites out of Egypt" (Exod. 3:10).

Moses was drafted, but Isaiah volunteered. His experience with God was as dramatic as Moses' encounter at the burning bush. Isaiah saw a vision of the God of glory in the temple and heard the voice of the Lord asking: "Whom shall I send? And who will go for us?" Isaiah volunteered: "Here am I. Send me!" (Isa. 6:8). A reluctant Moses wanted to argue with God's selective service system; Isaiah was eager to serve.

Samuel was just a boy when God began to speak to him and he began to hear. Amos was a grown man, pursuing his career as a shepherd and fruit cultivator, when God called him. Although he was neither a prophet nor the son of a prophet, he said, "But the LORD took me from tending the flock and said to me, 'Go, prophesy to my people Israel'" (Amos 7:15).

Jesus told His twelve, "You did not choose me, but I chose you and appointed you to go and bear fruit" (John 15:16). From time to time, God still taps someone on the shoulder for this special ministry. It is the responsibility of that one to hear and obey. Jesus says, "Come, follow me, . . . and I will make you fishers of men" (Matt. 4:19). He calls; we follow.

The call to ministry is more than a noble calling. Indeed, it is a glorious task, but a task it is. To be an "undershepherd" to the Great Shepherd of the sheep is wonderful work, but make no mistake: it is work! It might be a delightful duty to teach the people of God the deep things of God, but it is no light duty. Nor is organizing and mobilizing the soldiers of the Cross the work of a weekend warrior. Part of the burden of every pastor is the never-ending volume of work. There is also the burden of accountability to a high standard for the Lord's ministers. Look at what a pastor must be:

> Now the overseer must be above reproach, the husband of but one wife, temperate, self-controlled, respectable, hospitable, able to teach, not given to drunkenness, not violent but gentle, not quarrelsome, not a lover of money. He must manage his own family well and see that his children obey him with proper respect. (If anyone does not know how to manage his own family, how can he take care of God's church?) He must not be a recent convert, or he may become conceited and fall under the same judgment as the devil. He must also have a good reputation with outsiders, so that he will not fall into disgrace and into the devil's trap. (1 Tim. 3:2–7)

Some people compare this list with the demands on deacons in the next paragraph and see a double standard. Is there one level of expectation for pastors, maybe a little bit lower standard for deacons, and then a good deal lower standard for those in the church who are not leaders? That would be a triple standard. If one examines this list of standards for pastors and the requirements for deacons in verses 8–13, he should be impressed with the strong similarities. Then if one goes through the New Testament carefully, he would discover that virtually every requirement in either list is somewhere else required of every Christian. The possible exceptions are that a pastor should be "able to teach" and "not a recent convert."

There is no double standard in the New Testament. Yet the frailty of a member of the congregation may be tolerated in a way that it cannot be overlooked in the leader. That is the burden of accountability. It is no small part of our task. We should be able to say as the apostle Paul said to the Philippians, "Join with others in following my example, brothers" (Phil. 3:17). In explaining his actions to another church, he said, "We did this . . . in order to make ourselves a model for you to follow" (2 Thess. 3:9).

Likewise, Peter wrote to church elders to tell them how to shepherd God's flock under their care. He told them to be "eager to serve; not lording it over those entrusted to you, but being examples to the flock" (1 Peter 5:2–3). Every Christian will answer to God for leading anyone astray, but those who are charged with the task of church leadership certainly have a greater accountability. Yes, this noble task is a great responsibility.

Yours is also a multifaceted task requiring the development of skills of far-ranging variety. This book is sent forth to the beginning pastor or ministerial student with the prayer that it will help you get a grip on the many duties of the pastor.

In chapter 1, "Your First Pastorate," you should be able to identify some guidelines for discerning God's direction to a place of service. Or perhaps the Lord would lead you to start a church. How would you do that?

Chapter 2, "The Pastor Among His People," offers some direction on such pastoral duties as calling on members in their homes, in hospitals, and in the community wherever you find them. Chapter 3 is on "Pastoral Care and Counseling." What makes a good counselor? What principles guide a biblical approach to pastoral counseling?

Chapters 4 and 5 deal with "The Pastor's Pulpit Ministry" and one specific approach to pastoral preaching called "Problem-Solving Preaching." You will learn a step-by-step chronology for building a sermon, a survey of five methods of sermon delivery, and find help for long-range planning for pulpit ministry. Preaching to life situations is a special kind of pulpit ministry that a pastor would do well to master. The growing pastor will want to explore this approach and be alert to some great benefits and some notable hazards of this sermon genre.

"Pastoral Leadership" (chapt. 6) explores leadership styles with special attention to Jesus, our model. What is the pastor's role in leading public worship? How shall he guide the decision-making process of the church? How can he organize the church for advance?

Sometimes even God's people work at cross-purposes. A pastor needs to learn some "Conflict Management" (chapt. 7). How shall the pastor resolve his own inner conflicts? How shall he serve as peacemaker when members fall out with one another? And what shall the pastor do when he is the target of criticism and opposition?

Chapter 8 finds the pastor walking with his people in times of joy and sorrow—"Weddings and Funerals." The ministry of marriage, though joyful, presents some difficult decisions for the pastor. Should you unite a believer with an unbeliever in marriage? Should you bless the second or third wedding of those who are divorced? Should you require premarital counseling? And then there are mundane matters about how to ensure that wedding rehearsals run smoothly, and what policies a church should have for the use of its facilities.

The grief ministry is likely to be a stressful time, especially for the novice pastor. With a little forethought and a little experience, however, you will find it a wonderful opportunity to serve those who by sorrow are made ready for God's comforting Word.

Chapter 9 addresses two areas of "Ministerial Ethics." What ought a minister to do or not do when dealing with a church? And how does a pastor deal with his fellow pastors? Chapter 10 explores the special case of "The Bivocational Pastor." Some faith traditions believe every pastor should be bivocational; some do not allow it at all. If this is your calling, this chapter will alert you to some special blessings and some special burdens in store for you.

Chapters 11 and 12 take up the issues of "The Pastor as Teacher" and "The Pastor as Evangelist." A pastor need not excuse his neglect of these duties by saying, "I'm not gifted in that way." These are duties of the pastor, and they are disciplines that can be developed.

Chapter 13 offers guidance on both "Baptism and the Lord's Supper." These sacred ceremonies hold deep significance that pastors should understand and lead their congregations to appreciate.

"The Pastor's Stewardship of Time" (chapt. 14) gives the perspective of one who struggled mightily with this problem in more youthful years of ministry. I stayed with the pastorate long enough, however, to at least gain the upper hand against that dragon, if not to deal him a mortal blow. Here you will find some practical counsel for time management.

Chapter 15 offers scriptural guidance and the voice of experience on "The Pastor's Personal Life." Family matters, financial concerns, and spiritual formation are some topics covered here.

Welcome to the great adventure, dear pastor. May God use these pages to deepen your appreciation of your noble task, to equip you for this good work, and to encourage you in it. May you find great joy in the greatest of all callings. And when you stand before Christ, our final Judge, may you thrill at His smile of approbation and bow in grateful adoration to hear His commendation: "Well done, good and faithful servant!" (Matt. 25:21).

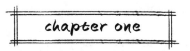

YOUR FIRST PASTORATE

ON A SATURDAY NIGHT IN 1890, a Baptist church in Whitewright, Texas, was in conference. The routine business was finished when the oldest deacon stood to speak. The frail old man began slowly and deliberately. "There is such a thing as a church duty, when the whole church must act."

A young lawyer in the congregation thought, *What a remarkable talk he is making. Perhaps he thinks it is his last talk.* But then he realized to his shock and dismay that the deacon was talking about *him*.

"It is my deep conviction . . . that this church has a church duty to perform and that we have waited late and long to get about it. I move, therefore, that this church call a presbytery to ordain Brother George W. Truett to the full work of the gospel ministry."

Someone immediately seconded the motion. Truett gained permission to speak. He urged them not to do this. "Wait six months, wait six months!" he begged. They would not wait. The congregation drafted him to be their pastor. Truett began at Whitewright, Texas, but in time became the distinguished pastor of First Baptist Church, Dallas.[1]

Most of us in the ministry have a testimony that differs from Truett's in two important respects. First, we are usually the first to know that God has called us to preach—not the last. Second, our problem is how to link up with the congregation where we may fulfill our calling.

This chapter will explore some of a minister's questions about the beginning of pastoral ministry.

HOW DO I FIND A CHURCH?

Or how will a church find you? Some denominations have a placement office. It might be the bishop in Methodist and other Episcopal traditions. It might be an executive office in the state convention or an associational missions director in Baptist circles. If you are in college or seminary, you probably will find an office there that seeks to match candidates and churches. If you are beginning as a bivocational pastor, a layman who knows you and respects you can help make contact with a church. In any case, your own pastor is one of the best resources. He will know of churches that are appropriate to gifts that he sees in you.

Meanwhile, volunteer wherever a preacher is needed. Start with a retirement center or nursing home near you. They will encourage you as much as you encourage them. Perhaps a nearby rescue mission needs volunteer preachers. Does the local jail or penitentiary have a chaplain? Volunteer to help. Teach a Bible class in your church. Get involved in your church's soul-winning effort. There is work to be done.

You will be doubly blessed if your first pastoral experience is as an assistant to a mature, seasoned pastor. An apprenticeship gives you opportunity to learn by example. There are a lot of things that seminary classes did not cover. For example, how do you conduct a staff meeting? How should you budget your time? What duties can you delegate and how?

HOW DO I KNOW IF GOD IS LEADING?

A study of the story in Acts 16:6–10 should be helpful in identifying some guidelines for finding the will of God. Paul and his missionary party came to an impasse at Troas on the coast of the Aegean Sea. Paul wanted to go on up the western coast of Asia Minor and enter the province of Bithynia. Somehow, the Spirit of God blocked this plan. While waiting, Paul had a dream. A man of Macedonia beckoned him to come on across the narrow passage and bring the gospel into Europe: "Come over to Macedonia and help us" (Acts 16:9b). Luke says that they concluded that God had called them to preach the gospel there. How did they reach this conviction? Five principles generally guide any believer in discerning divine direction:

1. *The Principle of Commitment.* God's leading is generally for those who are committed to follow. Paul and his companions were on a mission when God directed them to this new field of labor. God may occasionally reveal His will to a reluctant Jonah and then deal with his rebellion. But, as a rule, you don't pray, "God, if You show me Your plan for my life, I will give it consideration." No, first you yield to His will whatever it might be; then you ask for direction.

Some people look for direction from God about like Lord Nelson looked at the signal flags flying from the admiral's mast. In the Battle of Copenhagen, Lord Nelson put the telescope to his blind eye. He knew that the signal would tell him to come out of action, and he had no intention of doing so.

When you are committed to follow, you may expect God to guide. Abraham's servant went at his master's bidding to find a bride for Isaac. God led in a remarkable way to the home of Rebecca. Then the servant testified, "As for me, the Lord has led me on the journey . . ." (Gen. 24:27b). As a rule, God's guidance is for those on God's journey. As Paul wrote to the Romans, "I urge you, brothers, . . . to offer your bodies as living sacrifices, holy and pleasing to God. . . . Then you will be able to test and approve what God's will is—his good, pleasing and perfect will" (Rom. 12:1–2).

2. *The Principle of Communication with God.* Do you want to know God's will? Ask Him. Then listen to what He says. Prayer is our way of talking to God; the Bible is God's primary way of talking to us. In my youth, I remember someone saying, "God does not like to shout." If we want to hear His voice, we should remain within calling distance.

God made His will known to the centurion Cornelius at his time of prayer. He told him to send to Joppa for Peter. Then, while the messengers neared the gate, God made His will known to Peter as he also retreated to the housetop place of prayer.

3. *The Principle of Counsel.* Paul could be strong willed. If he thought that he had a word from the Lord, he acted. But in this case, he seems to have taken his companions into the decision-making process. Luke tells that "after *Paul* had seen the vision, *we* got ready at once to leave for Macedonia, concluding that God had called *us* to preach the gospel to them" (Acts 16:10, emphasis added). Paul was not alone in the decision. His missionary companions—Silas, Luke, and Timothy—seem to have had a part in discerning God's guidance.

Beware the pride of self-will that would go it alone. Even the Lone Ranger had Tonto. God knows that we need a community of faith. He places us in the fellowship of the church. From time to time, He brings special counselors into our crossroads experiences. Not all advice is good advice, of course, but "a wise man listens to counsel" (Prov. 12:15b). Blessed indeed is the young preacher who has a loving partner for life to whom to talk and with whom to pray.

4. *The Principle of Conscience.* The Holy Spirit of God prompts the sensitive conscience. He will disturb you when you lean toward a wrong choice, and He will give you peace when the choice is God's will. So Paul and his companions sailed across to Macedonia, "concluding that God had called us to preach the gospel to them" (Acts 16:10b).

Once, when I was itching to be relieved of a very trying pastorate, an opportunity came along that I thought must surely be God's answer to my prayer. A very wealthy man offered to set me up in a foundation that would assure me financial support. I could begin a traveling and teaching ministry. As soon as I told my wife the exciting news, she was suspicious. It turned out that she had good reason: The benefactor wanted me to arrange to turn the church I was serving over to him.

This is not to say that you should always "let your conscience be your guide." That slogan is not from Scripture. A poorly trained conscience is a poor guide. Nor is this a principle to be used in isolation. Instead, it is part of a pattern of divine leading, as is the next principle.

5. *The Principle of Circumstances.* "Paul and his companions traveled throughout the region of Phrygia and Galatia, having been kept by the Holy Spirit from preaching the word in the province of Asia" (Acts 16:6). How did the Spirit prevent that preaching? We do not know. It might have been through a disquieted heart or something more mundane, such as transportation problems or trouble on the border. Perhaps circumstances played a part. They came to one border and tried to move on, "but the Spirit of Jesus would not allow them to" (v. 7b). We would like to know how and why the Spirit barred the way, but we are not told.

It is frustrating to have your mind set in one direction and to find circumstances that block that way. But sometimes that is the way God leads. You might be approached by someone from a church. You pray about it and learn more about it. Soon, you feel sure that it is exactly where you belong. Your gifts seem to match the need there. Your heart tells you that it is surely God's will. But then the church turns its attentions to another preacher. They pass over you. The door seems to close.

One door closes and another opens. Do not take this to mean that *whatever* door opens before you is the one you should enter. But, after prayerful consideration, as in the case of Paul and his missionary party, you might find that to be precisely the leading of the Lord. It is good to remember that we are not blown about by chance winds of fate. A sovereign God works to open and close doors that He alone could know are best for His dear children.

WHAT INITIATIVE SHOULD THE CANDIDATE TAKE?

Not long ago, ministers considered it unethical for the preacher to take any initiative at all as a candidate for a pastoral call. He might pray about a place of service but talking to anyone else might be considered "playing politics." This is still a reality in some traditions, particularly where a district bishop makes appointments. Today, however, it is not uncommon for churches to advertise for applicants. Churches place ads in Christian magazines and newspapers just as do Christian schools seeking teachers and administrators. How much initiative, then, is appropriate? The answer to that question varies according to your denominational tradition.

We have already mentioned normal channels of contact between church and candidate. Talk to your pastor, assuming you have a trusted mentor or mature friend whose advice you respect. There might be a teacher or counselor who cares. Are denominational leaders in a position to recommend you to an available church? And don't forget active lay leaders in your church.

When you believe that you are ready for a pastorate, prepare a résumé. Identify yourself by name, address, education, and family data. Give a paragraph or two of personal testimony that will make clear your commitment to Christ and your sense of calling to ministry. List work experience, especially as it relates to your career objective. It would be well to list names, addresses, and phone numbers of a few respected persons who know you and can recommend you. Be sure to get permission in advance from anyone you use as a reference. Print your résumé on good quality paper.

Then what? Do you send the résumé to a pastorless church that you might like to serve? Some take that approach. Still, it is better if the résumé arrives from a third party, who will cover it with his own letter of recommendation. And, of course, those in an Episcopal tradition, a Methodist group for example, will contact the district superintendent or corresponding church official.

HOW DO I DEAL WITH A SEARCH COMMITTEE?

A church with a congregational government that is seeking a pastor will probably have a pulpit committee or search committee.[2] You will probably deal with a committee of five to seven leaders in the church before you meet the congregation. Be open and honest. Be yourself, but be your *best* self. The committee will probably ask many questions. If you are alert in listening to what they ask, you will learn a lot about the church. Often the questions reveal tension points in the congregation or perceived problems with a recent pastor. If asked,

"Do you work with all age groups?" you wonder, *Did the last pastor neglect the senior adults or the youth?*

"How much time do you spend in the study?" Hmm. That might mean, "Our last pastor didn't give much time to sermon preparation." Or it might mean, "He stayed in his study and never showed himself in the community." You may begin to wonder why they ask little or nothing about what you believe concerning the Bible. You wish that they would ask about doctrines you hold dear.

After giving candid answers to such questions, you should feel free to ask questions of your own and expect candor and honesty in return.

- What do they expect of a pastor? Do they have a written job description?
- What goals and aspirations does the church have? Do the lay leaders generally agree about the direction of the church? Do they have a written mission statement?
- How did the church relate to the former pastor? Do pastors typically have a long or a short stay in this church? Why did the last two or three pastors leave? Was it always an amicable parting? Do they have a committee or a board to supervise the pastor?
- What is the level of spiritual commitment in the church?
- What is the financial health of the church?

Financial matters should be the last thing discussed. You should not have to broach the subject. Probably the church has a policy or well-established precedent about the amount and method of paying the pastor. Is your health insurance and retirement taken from your salary? If you live and work in the United States, the Internal Revenue Service considers the pastor to be self-employed for purposes of Social Security taxes since (so far) the government is unable to tax churches. Churches should take this fact into consideration.

Shortly after I began my ministry in one church, a representative of the finance committee came to my study. He explained that it was church policy that the pastor provide an insurance policy that would spare the church the expense of long-term disability. I explained that I paid Social Security (at the self-employed rate) to meet that need. He was satisfied. Many pastors exercise an option to exclude themselves from Social Security. I read the government document. I understood it to state that I must be a conscientious objector to all such insurance plans. As a young man in robust health, I objected to the expensive premiums on financial grounds. And I questioned whether Social Security would remain an insurance plan or devolve into another government welfare system transferring the wages of the diligent to the less productive. But those were not allowable objections, so I paid Social Security premiums year after year. I doubted that the Social Security system would be solvent by the time I retired. Then one day a few years ago, I was up a ladder trimming tree limbs. I fell and sustained multiple fractures to my spinal cord. I was left permanently paralyzed from midchest down. My Social Security disability pension pays very little, but the medical insurance that comes with it is a lifesaver.

A pastor should take vacation time for the good of his church, his family, and himself. As other employers do, your church should grant two weeks of vacation (including two Sundays) after one year of service. If you stay four or five years, the church may grant a third week. You should not be expected to take your vacation time to attend training sessions, conferences, camps, and synods or conventions of your denomination. Certainly, if you take a group on a mission trip, you don't want to hear someone ask when you return, "How was your vacation?" The wise church will encourage such excursions by paying travel expenses as well as providing time away.

Most churches will be glad also if their pastor is invited to conduct a revival, an evangelistic meeting, or a Bible conference in another church. If they are pleased, they will grant the time away without taking it from your salary and without expecting you to pay for a guest preacher in your absence. Except in the most unusual cases, you should not schedule more than two weeks of such absences in one year.

Some pastors and committees want to treat all of these types of negotiations just as a business would. What's the *least* we can pay him?

Some pastors and some church lay leaders do not want to talk about money at all. My practice has been always to reach a decision before talking about pay. Maybe that was not always the best policy. For sure, it will not be the best for everyone.

WHAT ABOUT THE TRIAL SERMON?

The very term *trial sermon* makes us recoil a bit. The preacher is not on display, is he? Is the congregation merely sermon sampling? It was called "preaching in view of a call" where I grew up. Other parts of the country call it "candidating." We wish that another way existed. Appointment by a bishop seems so simple; we can all change places on a single Sunday. But a church with congregational government needs some way for the pastor and the people to determine if they are meant for each other. Presbyterian churches also elect teaching elders by congregational vote under their principles of republican government. This nearly always means a visit to the church, including a sermon or two.

Certain courtship protocols and courtesies are expected in dealing with a church. The following four deserve mention.

1. *Deal with one church at a time.* You might have a résumé in the hands of several committees, but when once you begin serious negotiations with one committee, let them be the *only* one. If another church comes calling, let them know if you are in the late stages of reaching agreement with another church.
2. *Deal only with a church that is dealing with only one candidate at a time.* If you find that it is a "horse race," politely bow out. If they ask you why, tell them that you do not wish to be in the competition. A committee might consider many potential candidates on paper, but when they begin interviewing, they should deal with only one at a time. They should let you know if they are moving on to other candidates. And they should never bring two or three candidates before the church in a kind of popularity contest. In such cases, some people will inevitably prefer one

candidate over another. If you are the one who prevails, you will then have the unenviable job of overcoming the disappointment of those who consider you their second or third choice.
3. *Decide if you will accept a call before a vote is taken.* It is most inconsiderate to let a church vote to extend a call to you while you are still shopping other potential pulpits. Also, if you are not ready to leave your current church, don't trifle with the affections of either congregation by pretending to be in search of God's will.
4. *It's best to vote the same day, in most cases.* Otherwise, some people will vote who did not meet you or hear you preach. And others who were there on the Sunday you visited will not be there for the vote. Also, a delay of only a few days gives time for church politics to get organized. This is not a healthful beginning for your ministry there. Nevertheless, some churches will want to wait until the next Wednesday or Sunday before they vote.

SHOULD I CONSIDER STARTING A CHURCH?

When I was a young preacher eager to serve, it hardly crossed my mind that I might be a church planter; more than a hundred churches of my own denomination were within an hour's drive of my home. Of course, many of them were small rural churches, and most of those were suffering declining membership. Family farms were fading away. Mechanization meant fewer hands were needed on the land. The jobs were in factories and shops in the growing cities. Sprawling suburbs needed new churches, but often that need was met by a church relocating from a declining urban core to the neighborhoods where their members were already moved.

Many of the little rural churches began to develop a maintenance mentality. I often heard lay leaders say, "Maybe our mission is to provide a training ground for student pastors." Somewhere along the way, we drifted from the New Testament pattern of church planting. Here at the beginning of the twenty-first century, some people are returning to that vision. It is a healthful sign. If you are impressed to explore church planting, think about the following points.

One thing *not* to do is to split a church. Don't encourage a splinter group. Although many new churches start from the broken fellowship of an old church, this is not the best. Paul and Barnabas disagreed sharply over whether to take John Mark on their second missionary tour. The result was two teams going in two directions. But notice how often Paul taught others to do better in his letters thereafter. "Let us therefore make every effort to do what leads to peace and to mutual edification" (Rom. 14:19). See also his words to the factious church at Corinth (1 Cor. 14:33; 2 Cor. 13:11). And note 1 Thessalonians 5:13: "Be at peace among yourselves" (KJV). But there are some things you can do:

1. *"Open your eyes and look at the fields"* (John 4:35b). Where is a church needed? What kind of ministry needs abound? Drive through a neighborhood that is without an evangelical witness. Do you see many tricycles and bicycles in the yards? Where there are skateboards and wagons, there are children. Maybe you can start with a vacation Bible school or a backyard Bible club.

Established churches rarely consider crossing racial or cultural divides. A population group might be isolated from the nearby churches by poverty, language, race, culture, or working conditions. Apartment complexes and mobile home villages often welcome attention of someone with a heart to meet their needs. When you find an unchurched group, what next?

2. *Gather a group of like-minded souls.* Perhaps it will be a community of young couples. They might be open to a Bible study group meeting in a home. If you arrange for child care at a convenient location and an affordable rate, they will be much more interested. Maybe a sponsoring church can provide this ministry at the church or in a neighboring home. You might meet one evening a week. Some people will drop out because it is not meeting their needs, but others will come to take their place. In time, a consensus will develop. When you outgrow a home, you might be ready for a rented space. Don't be too quick to buy property and put up a building; a church is *people*.

It might be better if you can start with a bang. If you have the resources to gather a hundred or more for the first meeting, you avoid a potentially crippling influence of those who are attracted to a small group because it is small. They might want to keep the new church a cozy little community.

3. It will often be wise for an established church to serve as sponsor. They will help to give doctrinal stability to the new flock. They might provide some needed financial backing.

4. The one essential to building a church is work—a lot of work. When Jerry Falwell was a young man just out of Bible school, a group of thirty-five people in his hometown were determined to start a new church. They asked the young preacher if he would stay in Lynchburg, Virginia, and help them. On Thomas Road, on the growing edge of town, they found a vacant property. It had been a hardware store and then a cola bottling company. They arranged to rent it for $300 a month with an option to buy.

Jerry decided that his first task was to knock on a hundred doors a day, six days a week. He took his Bible and a yellow legal pad for taking notes. When someone came to the door, he introduced himself and his purpose: "I'm Jerry Falwell. We're starting a new church up here at the bottling company building. I'd just like to invite you to come and attend our services!" The next Sunday, the attendance doubled. It soon doubled again. After a while, he enlisted a few men to take turns going with him. They learned to knock on doors. The attendance continued to double. It is now a church of more than twenty-two thousand members with a world-wide ministry. Brother Jerry, as he still likes to be called, is still training others to win souls and to plant churches.[3]

SHOULD I BE ORDAINED?

Spurgeon was never ordained. He called ordination "empty hands on empty heads." Nevertheless, there are good reasons for ordination. First, it is scriptural. That should be reason enough. In each letter that Paul wrote to Timothy, he urged him to give attention to his spiritual gift. And in both letters the apostle claimed that the gift came to the younger minister in the solemn ceremony of laying on of the hands of the apostle and others (1 Tim. 4:14; 2 Tim. 1:6). Paul and Barnabas were themselves set apart for their missionary calling by the Antioch church. Prayer and the laying on of hands were notable in that commission (Acts 13:1–3).

A second reason for ordination is very practical: it is important in civil law. You will be asked to conduct wedding ceremonies, for example. You will be acting as not only a minister of the gospel but also an official of the state in which you serve. Some states will require you to bring your license or ordination certificate to the courthouse, where they will enroll you in a book as one authorized by your church to officiate at weddings in your county or state. The federal tax code in America also wants to know who should be treated as a minister and who should not. Ordination (or its equivalent in other religious traditions) is a way to identify those who are, in fact, professional clergy.

Ordination is not only scriptural and practical but also traditional in most evangelical churches. That might not be reason enough by itself, but neither is tradition to be despised. The radical Reformers of the sixteenth century determined to throw out every tradition they could not fully and explicitly justify in Scripture. Other Reformers decided to remove only that which was clearly unscriptural. Tradition is not to be despised any more than it is to be enthroned.

I recently came across a 1743 treatise by Benjamin Griffith, titled "A Short Treatise Concerning a True and Orderly Gospel Church." Rev. Griffith was born in Wales in 1688. He came to America when he was twenty-two years old. The next year, 1711, he was ordained pastor of Montgomery Church in Bucks County, Pennsylvania, where he remained until his death fifty-seven years later. In his treatise, he said the following to a church about the ordination of ministers.

> After having taken all due care to choose one for the work of the ministry, they are, by the unanimous consent or suffrage of the church, to proceed to his ordination; which is a solemn setting apart of such a person for the sacred

function, in this wise, by setting apart a day of fasting and prayer, Acts 13:2, 3, the whole church being present, he is to have the hands of the presbytery of that church, or of neighboring elders called and authorized by that church, whereof such a person is a member, solemnly laid upon him, 1 Tim. 5:22, Titus 1:5, Acts 14:23, 1 Tim. 4:14, and thus such a person is to be recommended into the work of the Lord, and to take particular care of the flock of whom he is thus chosen, Acts 20:28.[4]

In this chapter, we have answered some of the questions asked by beginning pastors. We next will offer some guidance to the shepherd in how to care for the flock. "Keep watch over yourselves and all the flock of which the Holy Spirit has made you overseers. Be shepherds of the church of God, which he bought with his own blood" (Acts 20:28).

chapter two

THE PASTOR AMONG HIS PEOPLE

IN A LITTLE CHURCH ON A BAYOU in southern Louisiana, I once spent a week as the Bible teacher. I was a guest in the pastor's home. It was his first assignment after seminary. I soon found that he had a problem with timidity. He was so afraid of people that he could not make friends in the community. The Cajun people on that bayou were outgoing and friendly, but he stayed in the parsonage with the blinds drawn shut. He would lift a slat and peek out when someone went by. He did not last long in that pastorate. I wonder if he is still in the ministry. A pastor must work with his people as a shepherd does the sheep—up close and in person.

Jesus said that "the shepherd . . . calls his own sheep by name and leads them out . . . and his sheep follow him because they know his voice" (John 10:3–4). In a later chapter, we will emphasize the primacy of preaching and the need to spend time in the study, but let's learn here not to make what William Croswell Doane calls "The Preacher's Mistake."

The Parish Priest
Of austerity,
Climbed up in a high church steeple
To be nearer God,
So that he might hand
His word down to His people.

When the sun was high,
When the sun was low,
The good man sat unheeding
Sublunary things.
From transcendency
Was he forever reading.

And now and again
When he heard the creak
Of the weather vane a-turning,
He closed his eyes
And said, "Of a truth
From God I now am learning."

And in sermon script
He daily wrote
What he thought was sent from heaven,
And he dropped this down
On his people's heads
Two times one day in seven.

In his age God said,
"Come down and die!"
And he cried out from the steeple,
"Where art thou, Lord?"
And the Lord replied,
"Down here among my people."[1]

We might wish that all of the sheep would know when they are spiritually hungry and thirsty. Maybe they would come to church to be fed. Alas! If only it worked that way! The shepherd will need to spend much of his time going out to find the straying. Furthermore, those who are faithful to come to church will need the pastor's personal attention. The pastor will find himself spending a large block of his time calling on members. He needs to develop skill in three kinds of pastoral calls: (1) calling on the members in their homes; (2) visiting hospitals and nursing homes; and (3) making other calls in the community, such as to places of business, schools, and wherever people gather for leisure and recreation.

CALLING ON MEMBERS IN THEIR HOMES

Nothing will help a pastor get to know his flock like visiting in their homes. There he will learn more than names and faces. He will discover who is tempted to alcohol and other drugs and who is already trapped in addiction. He will learn who is morally crippled, who is nursing hurt feelings, and who is brokenhearted.

Someone will object, "But how can we visit our members in their homes? Both parents work; the children are in school. Should I give up my evenings with my own family? Anyway, the members don't want someone ringing the doorbell in the evenings; they are unwinding with their favorite television channel."

Yes, barriers must be overcome, but it can be done. And it is a duty. A plan for pastoral calls to the homes of members might include some of the following ideas.

1. *Start with senior adult members who are home all day.* They are often lonely. Perhaps no other group in the church will welcome the pastor as much as this group. Consider setting one or two afternoons every week for this visiting until you have visited each one. Try visiting by appointment. By grouping appointments geographically, one can make four or five visits in an afternoon. A visit of twenty or thirty minutes usually is plenty of time. If the people visited know that there is another appointment, they will not be offended by brevity.

Of course, some churches, especially rural churches, are composed almost entirely of senior adults. But these churches typically are small, so to visit every home is not an overwhelming task.

2. *Save evenings to visit those who are not available earlier.* Working families with school-age children need visits too. The day is past when the pastor could climb a fence and stride across the field to visit Farmer Brown on his tractor. Today, Mr. Brown works in the city in a factory, shop, or office. The boss would not smile at someone interrupting the work. Mrs. Brown also has a job. The children are in day care centers or in schools or with the babysitter. The pastor will have television for competition, but if he is to care for the flock, he will need to give at least one evening a week to house calls.[2]

3. *In some cases, Saturdays and Sundays are good days to visit.* My first pastorate was a student pastorate during college. The membership of that little rural church in the northwest corner of Louisiana was only about thirty families. The community had about that many more unchurched households. Faithful members of the church took turns providing Sunday dinner for my bride and me in their homes. The cycle took eight or ten weeks with some families inviting us more often than others. We spent the afternoons making pastoral calls and visiting the unchurched.

My second pastorate came while I was in seminary. Although that community was in Texas, it was remarkably similar to the first church I served. Either congregation was accustomed to having student pastors. Pastors did not live in the community but commuted. Either church provided hospitality for the pastor and his wife on Sunday. My pastorate in seminary also took care of us overnight on Saturday. Because neither church had a parsonage, we stayed in the homes of members. In a dozen weekends, a pastor could call on every home in the community. Your first experience might be similar. Those with a family should reserve Saturdays for them.

4. *Try informal get-acquainted times over a meal.* Some members of the church will invite the pastor out for a meal. Others entertain in their homes. It is easier to get to know someone in their own home. And there is an efficiency of time in using mealtimes for visiting.

The pastor who lives in the community might consider inviting members in for a meal at the parsonage. One pastor I know had two or three couples in at a time. You might suppose the major problem with this would be the financial burden. Imagine feeding the whole church. Actually, the bigger problem was not having enough evenings available for his plan. After a few months, many people still had not been invited, but they knew neighbors who had. They began to feel left out. The pastor had to publish details of his plan in the church paper with a plea for patience.

Surely, the pastor and his family deserve close friends. If it is impossible to invite everyone, don't let that stop you from inviting some people. As shepherd to *all* of the flock without playing favorites, the pastor still can have close friends.

I made a wrongheaded decision on this point in my first pastorate. We were having Sunday dinner with an elderly couple in the church. They told us that a former pastor had visited the community that week. He called on several homes, including her brother-in-law's family. "But he didn't come to see us." Over the next hour, I heard that sad refrain several times. Their hurt was plain also in sad faces and a distant gaze. I decided that I would never revisit the community after I was gone. I couldn't visit everyone, so I would not visit anyone. Later, I realized that this was a mistake. The only way a pastor can be equally close to everyone is to be truly close to none.

5. *Set visiting goals or quotas.* In a full-time church, one expects to have more homes on which to call, but also more days of the week available. Set a goal of how many homes per week to visit. Can you visit two hundred homes in your first year (in addition to calls on nonmembers)? Forty weeks of averaging only five visits per week will make two hundred visits. Many pastors do much more without neglecting other duties. When I was a teenage ministerial student, I was impressed by David M. Dawson Jr., who set himself a "par" of seventy pastoral visits a month.[3] I don't think I ever reached that number, unless I count hospital calls. Then it would often be more than seventy per week.

Some pastors will discover that they love to spend their time visiting the members. If this happens, rejoice and set some *limits*. You also have other work to do. The time might come when you will be senior pastor of a congregation of a thousand or more. Such pastors are not able to visit every home and still keep up with administration, weddings, and funerals.

HOSPITAL CALLS

Before the twentieth century, it was exceedingly rare to be a patient in a hospital. Then, early in the last century, hospitals multiplied. In the Depression of the 1930s, many hospitals faced financial collapse. No one had money to pay for services. Hospitalization insurance was just beginning. During World War II, hospitals became overcrowded. Still, most patients were there to give birth or to deal with a life-threatening surgery or other crisis. The pastor making hospital calls became as common as the doctor on his rounds.

By the last quarter of the twentieth century, people were going in and out of hospitals for elective procedures and tests of all kinds. Today, the pastor's visit is not always a crisis ministry. Still, hardly a better opportunity exists for a pastoral presence than the routine hospital call. Where else can the minister make three to five pastoral calls in less than an hour? Who needs to feel the shepherd's touch and hear the pastoral prayer more than one who is in a life-or-death crisis? Where will the pastor find greater joy than sharing the hour when a newborn baby blesses a young couple with its arrival? And what greater need exists for the pastor's reminder of God's promises than when a church family is visited by the death angel?

Following are some helpful things that I have learned about making hospital calls.

1. Make a brief visit. In a seminary pastorate, I often drove an hour or more to get to the hospital to visit one patient. In such a case, I thought that a five-minute visit before the hour drive back was hardly worth the trip. I'm sure now that I stayed too long for some of those visits. Unless the patient gives clear signals of needing the pastor for a longer visit, make it brief. Five or ten minutes is not too brief in routine visits.

2. Respect the hospital's rules and restrictions. Most hospitals welcome the minister as a valuable part of the healing team. However, some administrators and doctors resent pastors and restrict them. Whatever their attitude, a pastor is their guest. Don't interrupt the doctor in his or her duties. You can ask, "Should I wait outside or come back later?" Often, you will be invited to come on in. At other times, it will be better to visit another patient in the same hospital while you wait.

If the sign says "No Visitors," don't barge on in. Go by the nurses' station. Ask if you might leave a calling card with the nurse. Often, the nurse will say, "Oh, that sign is not for you. I think it would be great for the pastor to make a brief visit. Let me see if she is still awake."

To visit someone in "Isolation," all visitors might be required to "scrub up" and put on a surgical gown and mask and sometimes even shoe covers. This might be either for your protection or to protect the patient. In either case, start scrubbing. You might be God's man, but you are not God.

Pastors are often welcome to come at hours other than the posted visiting hours. It can be more convenient to avoid visiting hours and competition for the patient's attention with family and friends. But remember that these hours are filled with the coming and going of doctors, nurses, technicians, and aids. They come at pill time and mealtime, at bath time and "cath time." Remember, too, that those who are recovering might need a lot of rest.

3. Be sensitive to the patient's comfort. Stand where the sick one can see without twisting neck and head. Be careful not to bump the bed, IV rack, or monitors. Never sit on the bed—even if by invitation. Don't tell jokes to someone with fresh stitches. Speak in a soft but audible voice. If a hand is offered, gently take it but don't shake it.

4. Listen for cues that the patient might give. He or she might have bad news and want to talk it out—or not. I learned not to ask ladies, "What are you in for?" At least one of us might be embarrassed. You might ask, "Will you be here long?" Then they can tell as much as they want to tell. Nonetheless, you may learn more details than you want to know.

5. *Remember that you are a minister on a mission.* If you didn't have prayer when you first came in, do so before you leave. Sometimes the medical staff will be busy about the room, and it does not seem the time to invite them to pause and join in the prayer. Then take the patient by the hand, look him or her in the eye, and say something like, "My prayer for you is that you will know God's perfect peace as you go to surgery. May the Great Physician guide the hands and minds of the surgeon and all who labor with him." Or quote a prayer promise or other Scripture passage. "I know you are tired after all of those tests, and it's not unusual to have a little anxiety while you wait for the results. But remember the promise of Jesus: 'Come to me, all you who are weary and burdened, and I will give you rest'"(Matt. 11:28).

Early in my ministry, I decided to make Scripture reading a part of every hospital call. After all, I was a "minister of the Word." I had a coat-pocket-size New Testament with Psalms. I don't know when my routine slipped into a thoughtless ritual, but I know when I learned it was in that rut. I was visiting a young woman who was about to go to surgery to have a leg amputated below the knee. I had dropped into the habit of reading Psalm 121 at almost every hospital call. I came back to the real world that day when I read verse 3: "He will not suffer thy foot to be moved" (KJV). How I wish I had offered her Proverbs 3:5–6 or Romans 8:28—anything but that psalm.

It would be good to have a number of brief selections in mind. Better, list them in the flyleaf of your Bible. Following are some suggestions. Note that all of these relatively brief readings are from the New Testament or Psalms. You will, of course, add favorites of your own.

- Psalm 1
- Psalm 4
- Psalm 41
- Psalm 46
- Psalm 91
- Psalm 100
- Psalm 103:1–5

- Psalm 121
- John 10:1–5
- Romans 8:35–39
- 2 Corinthians 1:2–4
- 1 Peter 1:3–9

Notice that I have not included Psalm 23. It is a wonderful psalm—perhaps the most wonderful. Unfortunately, most people associate it with a funeral experience. That might not be the best medicine for a person in the hospital. I see some ministers going in and out of the hospital with big Bibles. There are some wonderful passages in the Hebrew Bible, but most hospitals have a Bible in each room that has been placed by the Gideons organization.

6. *You also have a ministry to family members.* One day you will be waiting with the family while the patient is in surgery. They know from the biopsy that there is a malignancy. Finally the surgeon comes, still in his scrubs, mask dangling under his chin.

"He came through the surgery. He's on his way to the recovery room. The tumor was metastasized. We got all we could. He'll be back in the room in an hour or so. Any questions?"

He looks at each family member in turn. No questions. Maybe a "Thank you, doctor." Out goes the surgeon. He's hardly to the elevator before they look at each other. "What did he say? What did he mean?"

Sometimes the family is too traumatized to ask a question. They might be overawed by the surgeon. In those times, you might help them: "Doctor Punjab, does that mean we should not expect a full recovery?" Keep in mind that terminally ill patients tend to block out mentally the news that they are not ready to hear. Family members sometimes do the same.

CONTACTS IN THE COMMUNITY

Besides pastoral calls in homes and hospitals, many opportunities exist in the community. Some of this visiting serves to become acquainted. Other visits build public rapport. But the true pastor is ready to encourage the discouraged and is searching for straying sheep. Here are a few ideas to consider.

1. Infiltrate the world of commerce. In some small towns, the pastor still can park on Main Street and go door to door. The hardware store, the barbershop, and the candy store—all are stocked with people who have spiritual needs. Some of them will be members of your church; others will not. Furniture and appliance stores, the café, and the corner service station—you need not buy anything to say hello and let them know you care. In the small town, the pastor will find a welcome.

In the city, attitudes are different. Someone who is not coming in to buy something is a disappointment. The typical urban stranger will be suspicious. "What's his racket? What does he want?" Even so, as you go about daily business, you will meet people. Ask the Lord to give a genuine love and sensitivity to spiritual needs. Christ can meet those needs through chance contacts.

2. Visit the schools. Court decisions seem to allow everything into public schools except Christianity. Nevertheless, opportunities exist. Make a point to meet the administration and faculty. Cultivate a special area of knowledge or expertise. A public speaker who has a message to youth about drugs will be in demand. So will one who has a message about honesty or sexual abstinence or racial harmony. Schools fight these battles every day. Even if a solution is Bible based, some public schools will welcome it.

Private schools are more open to a minister and his Bible. Many of them, however, will welcome only those with the affiliation of their sponsor. At least while a new pastor, include them all in a plan to get to know the community.

3. Are you interested in civic clubs? Personally, I never thought that I had time for Rotary, Optimists, or other service clubs. I had serious reservations about joining Masonic organizations or other secret societies. Other people might not mind swearing allegiance to a fraternity where much is kept in the dark. Some people make clubs and fraternities a substitute for loyalty to Christ. Some pastors, however, think that such memberships are great opportunities for service. Every man to his own Master must answer.

In my younger years, I served as a chaplain in the Civil Air Patrol. It was always a push to make the meetings. My main motivation for membership, honestly, was the flying time. I made some friends, but I don't know that I made a great spiritual impact on the squadron. It was my duty to speak to the unit periodically. They knew it would always be a Bible-based message. Where a pastor can minister the Word, the time and effort is not wasted.

4. *A hobby can open doors of ministry.* More pastors choose golf than any other form of recreation. Some of them find that it is the ideal time to combine exercise with the Lord's business. A pastor can make a foursome with members of the church he needs to get to know. For me, it took too much time for the relatively little physical exercise. It might be an expensive hobby too, although some clubs offer special rates to ministers. Other pastors get involved in coaching little league ball, soccer, or football. Coaches can make an impact on boys and girls for eternity.

As I entered middle age, I joined a health club and made physical fitness a definite part of my weekly schedule. I did so in the same spirit as my pastor friend Billy Crosby. He was into weight lifting. He had a muscle shirt printed with the words "Temple Maintenance" on the front. And on the back was the reference "1 Corinthians 6:19." That text says, "Do you not know that your body is a temple of the Holy Spirit, who is in you, whom you have received from God? You are not your own." Brother Billy did a good job of mixing ministry and muscle building.

5. *Consider a mission ministry.* Retirement homes and nursing homes are glad to see pastors. There may be a maternity home for unwed mothers where pastors may lead a Bible study or worship time. My earliest preaching experience was in such homes and in rescue missions and jails. The jail ministry was my most extensive experience and by far the most rewarding. In my first pastorate, professions of faith were rare. It might have discouraged me, except for the fact that I could preach the same sermon on Thursday in the local jail. There, days without professed conversions were rare indeed.

The shepherd cares for the sheep. In their homes, in the hospitals, and wherever else he finds them, he brings them Jesus. Sometimes, church members become acutely aware of a need for the pastor's counsel. Then they might come to you. The next chapter offers guidance for the pastor's ministry in the care of souls.

chapter three

PASTORAL CARE AND COUNSELING

NANCY CAME INTO MY STUDY before I had unpacked my books. She brought her husband and two-year-old daughter, but Nancy did all of the talking. She was really angry, and it was all my fault. She finished her tirade and stormed out. I was a bit shaken and more than a little bewildered.

Soon, however, I learned that the root of her anger had nothing to do with me or her complaint that day. She was dealing with a sentence of death from inoperable lung cancer. Over the next two years, we worked through that together. She came to accept her impending death. She made peace with God. And she accepted me as her pastor. In her last days in the hospital, she calmly outlined some things that she wanted at her funeral. She did not want her daughter, now four years old, to be there. She wanted me to explain to the little one after the funeral that Mommy was not coming back. That little girl is now a fine young woman who would make her mother proud.

Sharon and Dale were an attractive married couple. They were both highly regarded in the church. Dale was a deacon and a successful physician. Sharon came to see me one day brokenhearted. Through sobs, she told me that her husband had been unfaithful. He had become involved with a medical assistant in his office. In time, Sharon and Dale decided to try to save their marriage. He swore to his wife that the affair was over. She wanted him to come see the pastor, and he did, but if he had any remorse, he kept it well hidden. The last I heard, they were still together. I have wished that I had been a little more insistent that he deal with his sin.

Carolyn was middle-aged and single. She worked as a carpenter and could do about anything a man could do. She never had any boyfriends, but it did not seem to bother her. She did have a lot of baggage from childhood, however. In a number of visits over several years, she opened up about many things. An uncle raped her when she was a child and loaded her with guilt for his sin. She also told of being attracted to other women. She knew it would be wrong to yield to those temptations, however. Then she began to miss church. One day she came to the study to tell me that she would not be coming back to church. She had a lesbian lover who was moving in with her. I sadly reminded her of what she already knew about that choice. The affair lasted a couple of years and ended tragically. Carolyn still drops in on me unannounced, although I have not been her pastor for years. She still has a lot of baggage, but she is moving toward wholeness and learning that Jesus cares for her.

These are real case studies with names changed and the details altered enough to protect the privacy of the innocent and the guilty. They are typical of many cases of pastoral counseling. Not all stories are successes.

What is pastoral counseling? It is a person-to-person conversation in strict confidence in which the pastor seeks to offer a sympathetic ear and Spirit-led, Bible-based guidance to one who seeks such help. In this chapter, we consider some guidelines for this ministry, a biblical approach to pastoral counseling, and an evaluation of one model that might be helpful to evangelical pastors.

SOME GUIDELINES FOR PASTORAL COUNSELING

1. Be a good listener. This might be the best thing that you do. Before Sigmund Freud developed his theory of psychoanalysis, a troubled woman came to him for help. She told him that she believed he could help her if he would just listen. He did listen, day after day, as she told her story. In time, her problems went away. Freud called it "the talking cure." It might have been better labeled "the listening cure." One of my teachers, John Drakeford, wrote a helpful book for pastors, titled *The Awesome Power of the Listening Ear.*[1]

2. *Keep the ministry of reconciliation at the front of all you do.* Don't appear to be shocked by any confession, but do be nonchalant, either. The minister of Christ must not pretend to take sin lightly. People bring their burdens to the pastor for a reason, not simply because the pastor does not charge for a visit as does the doctor or secular counselor. They expect an honest appraisal of sin. They frequently may need to hear 1 John 1:9: "If we confess our sins, he is faithful and just and will forgive us our sins and purify us from all unrighteousness." Most counseling has to do with the healing of fractured fellowship. Sinful humanity's twin problems are alienation from God and estrangement from others.

3. *Remember that a shepherd is not a psychiatrist.* A counselor can quickly get in deep water, so learn when to refer the person to a mental health specialist. For example, a mother comes shortly after giving birth to her fifth child. She feels as though each arm and each leg weighs a ton when she tries to get up in the morning. She doesn't feel like cooking or cleaning or caring for children. That is not surprising. But then she says that she can't get away from the impression that her children would be better off dead. That is a scream for help, and she might need more help than you are equipped to give.

4. *Keep every confidence.* Counselors pass up some good sermon illustrations. The quickest way to lighten a counseling load is to go in the pulpit and say, "I had a couple come to my office this week. Their marriage is at the breaking point. He said. . . . She said. . . ." Would you take your burden to that pastor next week?

5. *Be aware of legal liability.* Fear of lawsuits cannot become an excuse not to help the hurting, but it should keep the counselor alert. In 1980, a woman brought a lawsuit against the Catholic nuns who operated a medical center in my hometown. The woman said that she had

found a snake in her bed. I don't think the court took her seriously. But, by 1985, clergy malpractice suits were in the news for real. The first wave was not accusations of sexual abuse by Roman Catholic priests. Rather, evangelical ministers were sued for various alleged failures in counseling. One disturbed young man went to the minister for help. The busy pastor gave him some teaching tapes. Later, he committed suicide. The parents sued the pastor.

Insurance companies are rushing to offer clergy malpractice policies. We are living in a very litigious society. It might take a few more years and a few more court decisions before we know if churches need such liability coverage. Sometimes the presence of a liability insurance policy *invites* litigation. For sure, the day when no one would think of suing the church is history.

6. *Guard reputation and character.* The New Testament standard for a minister is "above reproach.... He must also have a good reputation with outsiders" (1 Tim. 3:2a, 7a). At this writing, twenty states have made sexual or therapeutic deception by professional counselors a crime. Cases are being pursued vigorously against churches and pastors, as they should be. One notable case involved a pastor who was sued by one of his parishioners. The complaint included charges of clergy malpractice, negligent supervision, breach of fiduciary duty, and fraud. The pastor became sexually involved with a woman who was coming to him for help with her marriage. The suits were eventually settled by mediators according to state law. Large payments went to the offended family. Smaller payments went to the church and pastor. The great damage to reputations of all involved could hardly be calculated. And who will count the damage to the cause of Christ?[2]

The pastor must do more than keep morally pure. He must also guard his reputation. Give no room for rumors, nor step into a compromising situation. Conduct counseling at church as much as possible. I was blessed with an ideal setting in my last pastorate. The pastor's study had a whole wall of windows on one side opening to the outside. There was an outside door that sometimes accommodated those who did not want to come by way of the secretary. In the door to the hallway was an opaque glass panel. The secretary could tell if someone was in the room but not identify them. She could see, however, that we were on different sides of the desk.

The telephone in the pastor's study had a privacy switch. Even if the call came from outside, I could flip the switch and assure myself and the caller of privacy. No one could overhear in spite of many extensions around the church. People asked for that assurance often enough for me to know it was important to them.

7. *Remember that you have a "wonderful Counselor" as your helper.* Christ is our model for counseling. Study how He dealt with the Samaritan woman at Jacob's well, for example. But He is more. In the person of the Holy Spirit, He is present with us. What help we need, He supplies. When Jesus was about to return to the Father, He promised "And I will ask the Father, and he will give you another Counselor [of the same kind as I] to be with you forever—the Spirit of truth" (John 14:16–17a). It is an awesome task to be a pastoral counselor, but God does not leave us to do it in our own wisdom.

AN APPROACH TO PASTORAL COUNSELING

Sigmund Freud was an atheist. He lived from 1876 to 1939 but influenced modern counseling theory and protocol more than most ministers realize. He started psychoanalysis and psychotherapy. The first meeting of the International Congress of Psychoanalysis was in 1908. Alfred Adler, Carl Jung, and others joined Freud in this new approach to counseling. Freud advocated what would come to be called "nondirective counseling." The counselor never offers advice. He guides the conversation, usually with questions. Hopefully, the troubled person discovers the root of his own problem and decides on the best solution.

A biblical approach to counseling might follow the four imperatives of 1 Thessalonians 5:14: "And we urge you, brothers, warn those who are idle, encourage the timid, help the weak, be patient with everyone."

1. *Some people need warning or admonishing.* Jay Adams built his whole counseling method on the word translated "warn" in this verse.[3] It is often translated "admonish." He called it "nouthetic counseling,"

or "nouthetic confrontation," after the Greek word translated "admonish" or "warn." In the next topic, we will take a closer look at the Adams model for pastoral counseling. It has much to commend it. Note, however, that not everyone needs admonishing in every counseling session. The disorderly and unruly need to be admonished. The lazy need to be warned, but the pastor sometimes needs to guide gently.

2. Some people need comfort and encouragement. Sin is not always the problem with souls in distress. Thinking otherwise was the mistake of Job's three counselors. They admonished Job to confess and repent, when he really needed comfort and encouragement. Those who are "small of soul," as the original word suggests, don't need to be beaten smaller with a scolding; they need to be built up and given heart. Those who are spiritually and emotionally down need to be lifted.

3. Some people need the pastor's support and help. The verb in this command suggests the need to be loyal to someone, to hold on to someone, to help someone. The weak and the sick need this care. This phrase includes no thought of moral or spiritual defection. Such people don't need "nouthetic confrontation"; they need the pastor's strength in their weakness. Indeed, they need the pastor to help them find God's everlasting arms.

4. We must be patient with everyone. Jesus, our perfect pattern, was amazingly patient. True, He took a whip to clean out His Father's house of prayer. This was no sudden flare of bad temper. Notice how the gospel of Mark points out that Jesus came into the temple and looked around on the whole scene. He had seen it often enough before. Then He went out to Bethany for the evening. He came back the next morning with a plaited whip and cleaned house (Mark 11:11, 15). Jesus is very patient; otherwise, you and I would have been terminated long ago. Right?

It takes patience to see an alcoholic come to the end of his rope and finally reach out to Christ. It takes patience to help a couple save their marriage when both of them still think of love as something you fall into and out of. It takes a lot of patience to teach biblical stewardship to a population that has been brainwashed by Madison Avenue to be self-pleasing consumers. The pastor must be patient with everyone.

THE NOUTHETIC COUNSELING MODEL

With the reservations already mentioned, I commend the system of *nouthetic counseling* taught by Jay Adams. Adams was never trained formally as a clinical counselor. His doctorate was in speech. After a few years of teaching speech, he became professor of practical theology at Westminster Theological Seminary. In that post, he made a major contribution to the training of preachers. His writings reveal a man who is skilled in thinking "outside the box."

Adams's seminal book *Competent to Counsel* took its title from the Williams translation of Romans 15:14. "As far as I am concerned about you, my brother, I am convinced that you especially are abounding in the highest goodness, richly supplied with perfect knowledge, and competent to counsel one another." The first edition of Adams's book sold out in a few months.[4]

Adams challenged the Freudian approach to mental health care. Freud sought to correct poor socialization by expert psychoanalysis and psychotherapy. Nouthetic counseling, on the other hand, sees the basic human problem as rebellion against God. The only solution can be the resources of the Holy Spirit in the Word of God.

B. F. Skinner stressed "behavior modification," concluding that each person is a mess because of environment. If we can put the person in a better context, we can condition healthful thinking. Adams believes that changing the mind is the way to change behavior—not the other way around. People need meaning and hope. They do not gain this when the counselor gives them excuses for misbehavior. Instead they find wholeness when the counselor takes seriously their sin and alienation.

Adams also challenged the Carl Rogers approach. Rogers is the apostle of "human potential." He popularized encounter groups. Someone called his method "the group hug." Rogers was another advocate of "client-centered therapy." Adams, on the other hand, believes that the pastor must be very direct. If someone's behavior does not square with God's revealed standard in the Word, the pastor's duty is to point out that fact. Rogers thought that each person's basic problem is the failure to live up to potential. Adams, however, sees the problem as sin against God.

The Integrity Group approach of O. Hobart Mower also earned a challenge from Adams. Mower saw the central problem as bad behavior toward others. He wanted the dysfunctional person to draw on resources within self and the group for self-correction. Adams sees the basic problem as bad behavior toward God. The solution is repentance and faith.

Some counseling theories focus on insight; others focus on behavior. The pastor who is a serious student of psychology might gain useful insights from the study of any of these specialists. But he will do well to listen to the Word of God, as Adams has stressed. Because God breathed the Scriptures, they are useful to the minister. Those sacred writings will equip the pastor to set the norm for faith and life, to rebuke erring Christians, to set the crooked straight again, and to discipline in right living (see 2 Tim. 3:15–17).

SHOULD CHURCH MEMBERS BE REFERRED TO PROFESSIONAL COUNSELORS?

A pastor needs to know his limitations. He cannot be a specialist in all fields. Some outstanding ministers have been medical doctors. David Martyn-Lloyd Jones, who succeeded G. Campbell Morgan at Westminster Chapel in London, was a well-known physician. M. R. DeHaan was a medical doctor as well as a radio Bible teacher. Most of us do not have medical training. Nor do we have special knowledge about organic causes of psychological dysfunction. If you are not qualified to do surgery, you should not try it.

Sometimes you will need to refer someone to a specialist, ideally to a Christian practitioner. But as a friend of mine said, "If I need brain surgery and my choice is between an unskilled Christian and an expert pagan, I'll do my own praying and get the better surgeon." Other pastors and counselors disagree. Adams says, "Referral, except to another faithful shepherd, is out of the question."[5]

Sometimes referral is in the best interest of the pastor. Deep emotional issues might require a prolonged counseling relationship. It is not always just a matter of finding time for counseling. It is not uncommon for a troubled person to turn on the counselor with a huge load of repressed rage. They sometimes go public with their rage. The pastor cannot defend himself without betraying a confidence. He cannot even divulge that the angry parishioner has been in counseling. In addition, even successful therapy ends in loss to the caregiver. In many cases, such as depression, the counselee might form a dependence on the helping pastor. Healing is not complete until that attachment is broken. No shepherd wants to see his now healthy sheep move to another shepherd's fold.

A pastor who stays in one church and one community long enough will develop a network of trustworthy helpers. The pastor can refer to them with confidence. A man who called himself "Salvage Sam" had no connection to our church, except that he lived down the street and his toddler came to our Bible school. When he came to my office, he was trying to get his broken home back together. He told me also about his struggles to get a salvage business going. He had a truck and a trailer, and he had the large physique it took to dismantle old buildings and sell the scrap lumber and metals. However, he was not well capitalized. He planned to borrow the money he needed from a loan shark, who was going to charge him *10 percent interest per month!* I knew that two fine businessmen in our church had recently organized a small-business incubator. I arranged a meeting. They made a business arrangement.

The business consultant secured a line of credit from a regular bank with the understanding that the consultant-accountant would manage the money. The consultants taught Sam how to bid on city demolition contracts. They also helped him break an addiction to drugs. Meanwhile, I worked with him on his commitment to Christ and on trying to get his family back together. The last time I saw him, his business was doing well. He had a truce with his wife, though not yet a reconciliation. He was proud of being back in his son's life and determined to be a good father. Although he still was not giving much evidence of seeking God, he was very grateful for all of the help that God's people had given him.

We have not yet treated another method of pastoral counseling. Pastoral preaching may serve as effective group counseling. In the next two chapters, we will introduce the broad range of a pastor's pulpit ministry. In chapter 5, we survey the basics of sermon preparation and delivery. Sundays come around with relentless regularity. The following haunting line is in Chaucer's *Canterbury Tales:* "The hungry sheep look up and are not fed." God forbid that it should happen in your church. In chapter 6, we investigate a way to merge pastoral counseling and preaching. The shepherd who cares for the flock should seek to master the art of problem-solving preaching.

chapter four

THE PASTOR'S PULPIT MINISTRY

A FIRST-SEMESTER STUDENT called homiletics professor H. C. Brown Jr. at home one evening. The student had his sermon all prepared, except for one thing—the text. He summarized his outline over the telephone, then he asked if the professor might suggest a Scripture to go with this sermon. Dr. Brown suggested that he not turn in that sermon because it would surely deserve an *F*. Dr. Brown insisted on biblical sermons.

What is biblical preaching? It is not preaching *about* the Bible, nor is it merely preaching *from* the Bible. It is the faithful interpretation and effective application of Scripture in proclamation. "'Let the prophet who has a dream tell his dream, but let the one who has my word speak it faithfully. For what has straw to do with grain?' declares the LORD" (Jer. 23:28).

In this chapter, we suggest a step-by-step chronology for sermon building, then look at five methods of delivery that every preacher should try, and offer some guidance on long-range pulpit ministry planning.

SERMON BUILDING, STEP-BY-STEP

1. The sermon starts with selection of a text. What if an idea for a sermon comes before the text? What if the preacher needs to address a particular topic? Then the biblical preacher is not ready to begin sermon preparation until he has linked that theme to an appropriate text.

Ideas for sermons do come as the pastor sees needs among his people. He might notice a trend toward materialism, worldliness, or pleasure seeking in his flock. Certainly he should preach to meet such needs. Rather than pursuing one of these problems in a topical sermon buttressed with proof texts at every point, the biblical preacher will select a text and, as homiletician Wayne McDill likes to say, "let the text shape the sermon."

Plenty of ideas for sermons come to the pastor engaged in a program of ongoing Scripture reading and study. The beginner spends hours searching for a text. It is much better for the text to find *you*. It's more satisfying and it's safer. You are less likely to misuse a text that you discover in its context. We will say more later about a planned program of preaching that matches text and topic.

Remember that where you hurt, others do too. If you preach what *you* need to hear, you will often strike a responsive chord in other hearts as well. A pastor friend recently said from the pulpit, "Some of you struggle with depression and wonder if anybody understands what you are going through. God has taught me much about depression; I've been fighting that battle for years." He was overwhelmed by the sudden increase in his pastoral counseling load. The sermon idea might come from many places; sermon preparation really begins when that idea is wedded to a text.

2. After you've selected the text, interpret the text. Before you open a commentary, analyze the passage for yourself. Find the "Big Idea," as Haddon Robinson calls it. How does this idea fit into the context of the whole book of which it is a part? Make notes of your findings. The closer the "big idea" of your sermon matches the "big idea" of the text, the more biblical the sermon will be.

Use sound principles of interpretation. Orthodox theologians generally agree on a number of principles for *hermeneutics*—interpreting Scripture. These principles are usually identified as the "grammatical-historical method." I prefer the term that some people are using now, the "historical-theological method." By understanding the Bible's redemptive message to people *then*, we are able to recast and share its message *now*. The interpreter who follows sound principles of interpretation will recognize the priority of the original languages. We will expect a progressive revelation; the New Testament stands at a more mature level than does the Old. Another rule is that "Interpretation is one; application is many." You will find other rules or principles in a good hermeneutical textbook.[1]

The neglected principle of hermeneutics is the "spiritual principle." Samuel Taylor Coleridge said, "The Bible without the Spirit is a sundial by moonlight." Nineteenth- and twentieth-century theologians rejected the idea that Holy Scripture required the aid of the Holy Spirit to enlighten the interpreter.[2]

The spiritual principle of hermeneutics has four points:

1. *The interpreter must be born of the Spirit.* "The man without the Spirit does not accept the things that come from the Spirit of God, for they are foolishness to him, and he cannot understand them, because they are spiritually discerned" (1 Cor. 2:14). Jesus told Nicodemus, "I tell you the truth, no one can see the kingdom of God unless he is born again" (John 3:3).
2. *The interpreter must be willing to submit to the Word as well as understand it.* "If anyone chooses to do God's will, he will find out whether my teaching comes from God or whether I speak on my own" (John 7:17). The interpreter must be continually yielded to the Holy Spirit because some truth is available only to "the spiritual man [who] makes judgments about all things" (1 Cor. 2:15a).
3. *The interpreter must grow by practice and exercise.* Babes in Christ can digest the milk of the Word. "Solid food is for the mature, who by constant use have trained themselves to distinguish good from evil" (Heb. 5:14).

4. *The interpreter should pray for spiritual illumination.* Our prayer should be that of the psalmist who sang, "Open my eyes that I may see wonderful things in your law" (Ps. 119:18). James reminds us that if we lack wisdom we should ask God, who gives it (James 1:5). And Paul prayed for his Ephesian friends that God would give them the "Spirit of wisdom and revelation" so that they would know God better (Eph. 1:17–18). This is the neglected principle of biblical interpretation. Although it is clear and prominent in the New Testament, it hardly ever is mentioned in textbooks on hermeneutics, including those by evangelical writers.

So, prayerfully and diligently come to your own best understanding of the text. Then go to reference books and see what other scholars have to say about the passage. Make notes on what you learn from commentaries, word studies, and other Bible study tools. When you are confident and clear in your interpretation, write out the central idea of the text. Put it in a single clear sentence. Until the idea is clear to you, you will never make it clear to your congregation. The test of your understanding is how well you can craft this statement of the central idea of the text.

This is a good time also to decide on a goal for the sermon. If you don't know what you hope to accomplish and state it clearly on paper, you are not likely to take anyone along to any destination.

3. Gather materials. A sermon is basically interpretation and application. But you also need supporting material. This stage of gathering material often overlaps with the stages of maturing and organizing. For the sake of distinguishing each function, however, we will treat each separately.

A sermon needs illustrations. Unless the text itself is a story, the sermon will need narrative quality. Jesus told parables and other stories. They made His message both plain and portable. Children love stories, and so do the rest of us. Television and movies have made us more right-brained, inductive thinkers than were earlier generations. Illustrations help the preacher clarify his meaning. They also promote persuasion by showing how a Bible truth can apply to modern life. Young and old, rich and poor, simple folk and sophisticated—everyone appreciates a good story.

Use illustrations from nature and science, biography and history, poetry and art. Be very careful about using too much personal experience. And the preacher should never glorify himself in his sermon. Any use of your own pastoral visitation or counseling experiences is likely to be unwise. Avoid the published collections of preachers' anecdotes. They were probably all worn out before the book went to press.

The question arises, How do I save sermon illustrations and other support material? Some preachers use memory alone. A preacher friend of mine uses humor in the pulpit much more than I do. When he hears a good story, he looks for someone to tell it to as soon as possible. This helps to fix it in his memory.

I am a fanatic filer. I have thousands of four-by-six-inch note cards filed by text and topic. Other preachers use scrapbooks, large envelopes, file folders, or just a pile in a drawer. You can simply mark books in your own library. If you use the card file system, you can index your library by text and topic. If you would you like to see a sample of an indexing card form I developed, write to me using the contact information found elsewhere in this book. I also use four-by-six-inch file cards for pulpit notes. They are easy to organize. Flip them over on the back. On the top line, enter the text and title. Under that, note the date and place you preached it. But back to sermon preparation.

4. *Allow the mixture of materials to mature.* You will be happy to know that you have ten thousand million brain cells. They rest neither day nor night. If you start your sermon early enough, they will help you build it. Andrew Blackwood was the dean of homileticians. His book *The Preparation of Sermons*,[3] fortunately for me, was the first such book that I read as a seventeen-year-old looking for help. He began a fifteen-step procedure for preparing a sermon with the following maxim: "Allow abundance of time for the sermon to grow." A later step also called for a time of incubation for the material. It takes time to produce an oak tree, and a solid sermon will not grow up like

Jack's bean stalk overnight. Start early enough to let the seed germinate, grow, and ripen into maturity. Your subconscious mind is at work mostly when you relax.

Working some on the sermon every day promotes this process. When you are driving to make a visit, when you are counseling, and when you are mowing the lawn at home, your mind will keep working on the idea. Thoughts will push from the subconscious into the conscious mind. If you keep a folded note card in your pocket, you can catch the fleeting idea and focus on it. When you jot down a concept, it will begin to sharpen and expand. The human brain is more efficient than a powerful computer in problem solving. It takes time to build a sermon.

5. *Organize the material.* As the mass of material begins to accumulate, you should notice that it lacks structure. A trial outline might present itself long before you have gathered all of the material. Don't rush into structure until this sermon's subject is clear. Perhaps you are working on Mark 2:1–12, the story of the bedridden man whose four friends brought him to Jesus. As your study progresses, you decide that the authority of Jesus to forgive sins is the central focus of the passage.

Suppose that someone asks you, "What are you preaching about next Sunday?" You might say, "I'm going to preach on forgiveness of sins." But what if they ask next, "What are you going to say about it?" You should have a one-sentence answer: "Jesus Christ has the authority to forgive you of all of your sins."

You should also have a clear goal in mind to tailor a sermon to a particular congregation. Halford Luccock, a great American preacher and homiletics teacher of the early twentieth century, told of a theological student who went to preach in a church that he had never visited. When he came to the pulpit, he was confronted with a neatly framed card displayed in the preacher's direction. It asked, "What are you trying to do to these people?" That question rather distressed him as he ran over his sermon mentally. He had to admit to himself that he had no specific goal in mind for his sermon. He was just preaching![4]

Organization helps the preacher clarify and remember his own thoughts. It also helps the hearer follow and remember the message. Listeners will not tolerate the frustration of not knowing where you are taking them. They will tune you out if you seem to be wandering in a field. Mentally, your hearer will say, "I'll go sit on this fence rail while he makes up his mind where he wants to go."

What kind of organization should a sermon have? John Broadus said that the qualities of a good sermon plan are unity, order, and proportion. The parts, taken together, must equal a whole. And the parts must relate to the whole by some specific design.

6. *Write and rewrite the sermon.* I can hear the complaints already: "I don't like to write sermons. I can't write a sermon. I do better preaching from an outline. My sermon sounds artificial if I write it out."

Yes, yes, I've heard it all before. But at least for the first few years of your preaching, you need the discipline of writing sermons. If you don't believe me, try the following experiment. Take a tape of one of your sermons as preached. Ask someone to transcribe it word for word on a word processor. Then see how it reads. If that doesn't convince you, try another experiment. Stand in front of a mirror. Look yourself in the eye and ask, "Why are you so lazy? Don't you think you should do your best in handling the Word of God?"

When you write a sermon, you will be tempted to start with the introduction. No, write the conclusion first. Embody in a strong conclusion the purpose upon which you have already decided. Call for decision. Then write the body of the sermon, moving in a straight line toward that goal. When all else is written ("The last shall be first"), write the introduction.

Plan to finish writing early enough that you can let some time elapse before revising. At least leave it alone overnight. Then start rewriting. Your introduction is two pages of a ten-page sermon; that's too long. Cut out one page. The first of three sermon divisions takes as much space as the other two divisions combined. Chop, chop. Restore proportion. You notice that you have said "finally" as you begin the last sermon division. But you have five pages ahead of you with this division and your conclusion/invitation. The congregation will think you're a liar.

If you are fortunate enough to have secretarial help, dictate your rough copy and see how it transcribes. I once had a secretary with limited vocabulary. At first, it annoyed me that she misunderstood so many words. Then I saw it as a blessing. If she did not understand some of my theological jargon, many others in the congregation would miss my message too. Whatever else the sermon is, it must be clear. Make it clear enough for the children, and maybe the adults will get the point.

Dictation also solves the problem of sermons that sound like essays. Studies with stroke victims have shown that one's oral vocabulary and speech patterns do not come from the same part of the brain as the written vocabulary and style.

Charles Allen was an outstanding communicator who served Methodist churches in Atlanta and Houston in the mid-twentieth century. When he wrote his sermons, he first spoke each sentence aloud. Then he wrote it down in longhand. When he finished writing, he almost never changed a single word on the paper. He preached with a welcome clarity and simplicity of style.

Check more than style, however. Ask some content questions. Does this sermon honor Christ? Does it call for a change in the life of the hearer? Does it proclaim God's Word or the word of the preacher? Does the message matter? We would change a lot of the things we say and do if we judged them by one question: What difference will it make a hundred years from now? More than anyone else, the shepherd of souls must keep eternity's values in view.

LONG-RANGE PLANNING FOR THE PULPIT

Rev. Clueless is a procrastinator. Every week he goes through the same scenario. He spends Monday in a depression because he did such a poor job preaching on Sunday. Then on Tuesday, Wednesday, and Thursday, he goes about his pastoral duties, trying to forget that Sunday is coming again. By the weekend, he is desperate for an idea for a sermon. Any idea! He spends two or three hours flipping through his Bible, hoping that a text will jump out and rescue him. He prays with desperation, begging, promising to do better next week. But it seems that the heavens are brass. Finally, aware that time is running out, he pulls down *Simple Sermons for Simpleminded Ministers* and selects one that he has not yet offered his congregation.

There is a better way. It involves long-range planning. Besides easing the pressure of deciding what to preach next Sunday, the advantages of this method are many. To know the sermon schedule months in advance allows time to gather material, organize, and prepare. You don't waste hours trying to get started. The text and tentative topic are in place. Also, planning gives more balance to pulpit fare. Sermons can come from both the Old Testament and the New Testament. The flock can feed on the Gospels, the history of the expansion of the church in Acts, and all of the letters. By planning in large blocks, the preacher can see at a glance if Paul's letters are used to the neglect of Peter, James, and John.

Planning for the pulpit also helps planning for the worship service. Music can complement the sermon theme. Baptism and the Lord's Supper can be a vital part of a worship experience and not just an appendage. Once you adopt this discipline, you will never go back to the old way.

Here is how to do it:

1. *Decide what your congregation needs.* Certainly a generous amount of evangelism should be in the plan, even if it seems that nearly everyone attending is already a believer. Christians also need to hear the gospel.

They have other needs too. People are lonely and need assurance that they are not alone. They are tempted and need help to overcome. They bear grudges and have trouble forgiving. They have doubts, dreads, and disappointments. They might be well educated and more mature spiritually than are people in any other church you know, but they still need instruction in Bible doctrine. Such ethical issues as gambling, race relations, and honesty in business confront them daily.

Start your own list of needs as you pray for your flock. That list will get longer, the longer you serve that congregation.

2. *Plan a year at a time in three-month blocks.* I discovered that

January to December is not a good cycle for me. I found that I was always spending large blocks of time getting ready for a Bible study scheduled in January. It worked better to plan twelve months beginning in April.

You might decide that you are going to spend the time from Christmas to Easter preaching through the gospel of Luke or John. Or you might follow the life of Christ from a harmony of the Gospels. Preaching the life of Christ might well take several months, although five to seven sermons in one series would be better for most topics. This year, you might plan a series on the parables of Jesus and next year a series on the miracles of Jesus. John's gospel seems to be organized, at least in its first half, around a series of seven "signs" or miracles of Jesus, beginning with the turning of the water into wine and climaxing with His raising of Lazarus from the dead. The rest of the gospel is the story of the Lord's last days in Jerusalem.

By planning sermons in series, you make your study time more efficient. Suppose that you decide your church needs to focus on the Ten Commandments. You label ten file folders and start to work several months in advance. Each book you read and each commentary you research will provide help for all ten sermons. Newspapers and magazines will suddenly seem to be overflowing with examples of breaking the commandments. The same thing happens when you preach a series of expositions through a Bible book.

Suppose that you want to preach through Esther. It has ten brief chapters. Each might provide the text for an expository sermon. After learning all that you can about the book as a whole and all of its parts, you might come up with a series such as the one displayed here.

EXPOSITION OF ESTHER

Chapter 1   The focus is on Queen Vashti. The message to your congregation is about living with conviction. When you face the hard moral choices of life, may you have clear convictions and the courage to stand on them whatever the cost.

Chapter 2   The focus turns to King Xerxes and his rash decision to end his marriage with Hadassah. By planning all ten chapters in advance, a preacher can decide whether to focus on the theme of divine providence in this chapter or wait until chapter 6. This is a good text for encouraging marriage stability. Consider the subtheme: A good woman is hard to find.

Chapter 3   Haman the Hateful takes center stage. You can be sure that some people in your congregation also are trapped in hatred of others. Haman's hatred began in pride and moved to uncontrollable rage. This chapter does not resolve the problem, so the preacher might decide to look ahead to chapters 5 and 7. Or pair this story with a New Testament text on love.

Chapter 4   Esther decided to go in to the king although it was against the law. "And if I perish, I perish." Consider the case for civil disobedience in this story. How does one know when to obey or disobey government? And how much civil disobedience is right and proper?

Chapter 5   Haman is again on center stage. You might decide that this is a great text for a sermon on the poison of resentment. It robs one of joy, and it infects other people. Ultimately, it will destroy the hater.

Chapter 6   This chapter is a wonderful case of the amazing providence of God. The tables are turned on the villain, and Mordecai is rewarded. God's timing, His strategic placing of people in our paths, even little things that seem to be accidental are in God's sovereign control.

Chapter 7   This chapter returns to the theme of hatred. If you are planning, you will notice that fact. You might decide to focus on racial prejudice as a form of hatred in a sermon on building your own gallows.

Chapter 8   The theme of this chapter is putting an end to evil plans. It is not easy to change the momentum of evil once set into motion, but we must do so. And we must depend on God to see that evil plans do not prevail.

Chapter 9   The tables are turned in this chapter. Your sermon might focus on celebrating God's goodness without becoming vengeful and vindictive.

Chapter 10   Mordecai again takes center stage. This text can encourage self-giving service as a lifestyle. Mordecai was not grabbing for the spotlight but working offstage. It was not luck but labor that made the big difference. He did not advance by compromise but kept his character and his convictions true.

3. Keep the church calendar in view. Some churches expect the minister to follow the Christian year—Advent, Christmas, Lent, Good Friday, Easter, Whitsunday, and Trinity. Holidays and holy days. Easter, Thanksgiving, Christmas. You don't have to observe every date on the liturgical or denominational calendar—much less every tribute invented by the marketers of greeting cards. One pastor in a new charge was criticized because he preached on the Sunday before Memorial Day, never mentioning the holiday coming up on Monday. He didn't even recognize the veterans in the church. The offended veteran who aired the complaint was conditioned by that church's recent traditions to expect certain strokes every year on that Sunday.

Some pastors follow a published lectionary that selects the text for each Sunday. That might be a good discipline. It does save a lot of time selecting next Sunday's text. It ensures that the preacher will cover the whole gospel and almost all of the Bible over time.

Some people will object that long-range planning does not allow for the leading of God's Holy Spirit. I will say two things about that objection. First, God knows better than we do what lies ahead. I have marveled more than a few times at the "coincidence" of a text and topic chosen weeks in advance. When the day came to preach, that topic was exactly what was needed to meet a need that no one could have predicted. Second, there is no reason why plans cannot be changed to meet a need that arises. I'm sure that a lot of sermons were modified on the Sunday after the tragedy of September 11, 2001.

I once took a group of young people on an all-day outing to a state park. The friend who organized and promoted it planned a youth rally for the evening. He reserved an open-air amphitheater. He also invited a youth group from a religious tradition quite different from that of our youth. It was a noble undertaking; he hoped that we could all meet on common ground and celebrate Christ together. A problem arose, however. Because no one was clearly designated to be in charge, the guests from the strange tradition took over. Our young people had never seen such a frenzy of jumping up and down and falling out on the ground. That was Saturday evening, and by Sunday afternoon I was wondering if I should change my preaching plan. Another text and another message crowded in to take the place of the one I had planned. I decided to put it to the congregation to decide. I don't remember what my original plan was, but when I offered the choice between that one and a message on "Emotion in Worship," there was no doubt which one they were ready to hear.

FIVE METHODS OF SERMON DELIVERY

Every preacher will need to find his own best method, but all five of these methods of delivery are worth trying. You might think that you know which is best. But you do not know if you have not given all five methods a fair trial. And that means trying each more than once or twice.

1. *"Free Delivery" is preaching without any notes at all.* The preacher may prepare a full manuscript, but he does not bring it to the pulpit. Nor does he use even a summary outline. Some men, like the late W. A. Criswell of Dallas, mark cue words in their Bibles and put key words in the margin. Clarence E. Macartney prepared his manuscript but took to the pulpit no notes at all. T. DeWitt Talmadge, after a couple of early embarrassing attempts to use his manuscript, began to preach without notes.

Andrew Blackwood said that free delivery was the only style of preaching until after the Reformation. It certainly has the advantage of better communication with the audience. Laymen who could never make a speech in public with or without paper, appreciate a pastor who can preach without notes. It will not work for every preacher, however. The pressure of doing it right is more than some people can bear. A friend and colleague who is a very effective professor of preaching requires all his students to learn to preach this way. I once asked him how they like this requirement, and he admitted, "They hate it."

2. Memorizing a manuscript allows natural delivery. Pulpiteer R. G. Lee (1886–1978) was an oratorical master of this method. He wrote all of his sermons with a pen, taking care to paint word pictures with vivid imagery and plenty of action. His secretary typed the manuscripts in those days before word processors. He read them over several times, picturing the words. Then he preached just as he had written it, usually without notes. Thomas Guthrie (1803–1873) was perhaps the greatest platform speaker of his time. He memorized his sermon, but his delivery was so natural that it seemed extemporaneous. John Angel James (1785–1859) was a British Congregationalist. He preached fifty years at Carrs Lane before R. W. Dale succeeded him. Dale witnessed a sermon of fifty pages that lasted two hours. James delivered it from memory. The preacher's brother sat nearby with the manuscript in case James experienced a moment of hesitation. He didn't. Except for a few minutes rest at the end of the first hour, he did not change so much as a preposition from the manuscript. Certainly James had a remarkable gift. Others who memorized their written sermons were G. Campbell Morgan, Billy Sunday, Dwight L. Moody, and Wilbur Smith. Some of those men soared to rhetorical heights using this method.

In spite of so many pulpit giants who have memorized their sermons, the downside to this approach is significant. The memorization process consumes much time in preparation, and the task is a great mental burden for ordinary mortals. The fear of forgetting might actually cause the dreaded "blackout." Some men cannot do it without seeming artificial. And the delivery might come across as more recitation before the congregation than communication to them. Some preachers who are reciting from memory avoid eye contact lest it derail them, and that habit does not help communication.

3. Reading a manuscript has little to commend it, but it might have a place in the pulpit. Please understand me: I strongly recommend preparing a manuscript. I don't recommend reading it to the congregation. I have already stressed the discipline of writing sermons. At least for the first five years of ministry, make yourself do so. If you preach two or three new sermons a week, I admit that it is a counsel of perfection. And I admit that most of the time I managed one polished manuscript for Sunday morning, one less polished sermon brief for Sunday evening, and an outline for Wednesdays.

Outstanding preachers who did preach from manuscript include Phillips Brooks, George A. Buttrick, and Alexander Whyte. Jonathan Edwards sometimes read his sermons in a monotone with the paper held close to his nose because of his poor eyesight. Yet what powerful sermons they were, and what power of the Holy Spirit attended Edwards's pulpit ministry.

John Henry Jowett, Thomas Chalmers, and Peter Marshall used manuscript delivery. Billy Graham found that in the early days of live radio and television, producers required it. If you preach on live broadcast or telecast, you might still find that you must have a manuscript. The station manager is bound by the fairness doctrine that requires him to provide free airtime to anyone who seems to be attacked by your sermon. Certain academic settings will also require a manuscript reading. But unless it is read so well that no one knows it is being read, the manuscript becomes a barrier to communication. Spurgeon, in *Lectures to My Students*, compares the preacher's up-and-down head movements, as he looks from manuscript to audience and back, to the bobbing of a hen drinking water.

The method has its advantages. It can keep you from embarrassing mistakes. A guest preacher in my pulpit was preaching on Paul and Silas in the jail at Philippi. He said not once but three times, "And there they were in stocks and bonds." He probably would not have written that line. Or, at least, he would have revised it before preaching. Another preacher was waxing eloquent on "All have sinned and fall short of the glory of God" (Rom. 3:23). He pointed to the congregation and asked, "How many of you are tired of always falling short? Well, I've got news for you. Christ has redeemed us all from our falling shorts!" His wife laughed so hard she almost fell out of her chair.[5]

The manuscript also can be timed precisely. A well-prepared manuscript has no unfortunate omissions or rambling repetition. It is much better to cut three pages from your manuscript in the study than to try to decide what to omit in the pulpit when your time is about expired.

The objections to manuscript delivery all deal with the reading of it. A preacher may prepare a manuscript and preach either without notes or with only an outline. One may also use his manuscript as pulpit notes. When for several years I served a church with two morning services, I found the manuscript to be a big help. It saved me from the distressing thought: "Did I just say that, or was that in the earlier service?" If you use your manuscript for pulpit notes, don't turn the pages but slide them. If you have two pages at a time side by side, you only have to do that four times in a ten-page manuscript. Use a highlighter to mark key words and sentences.

4. *Extemporaneous delivery calls for mastering the subject but not writing a manuscript.* With this method, the preacher uses brief notes, usually an annotated outline for delivery. In the days of typewriters, I used a single four-by-six unruled index card. As word processors replaced typewriters, I found a single letter-size sheet folded to Bible size worked well. Extemporaneous delivery is the most prevalent method used in the pulpit today, and it is the most widely recommended. Charles H. Spurgeon almost never composed a sentence in advance. He studied a number of texts for weeks. Each Saturday evening after supper, he retired to his study and selected the one that was most ready for delivery. This was also the method of Joseph Parker, Spurgeon's crosstown contemporary at London's City Temple. The list of outstanding extemporaneous preachers is long and includes George W. Truett, Alexander Maclaren, John Calvin, and Robert W. Dale.

Extemporaneous delivery has the advantage of saving the time that writing requires, yet the notes help set the mind at ease. The preacher has a plan to follow but can think on his feet and adjust to his hearers. Notes will help with quotations, statistics, poetry, and Scripture cross-references. Extemporaneous preaching certainly is more natural than reading or memorizing the sermon.

To speak well extemporaneously is not easy. Most sermons will suffer from little attention to rhetorical style. The choice of words might tend to be trite and repetitive. Just as a manuscript can get in the way, so can notes. And one of the biggest drawbacks is that when the notes grow cold, they usually are of little value. Sometimes the notes grow cold between the study and the pulpit. Is there any preacher who has never come to a line in his notes and wondered, *What in the world did I mean by that?* "Story of little boy and dog." What little boy? What dog? What story?

5. *Impromptu preaching is preparing the mind without using paper.* This is not the same as unprepared preaching. Charles G. Finny did not believe in writing out his sermons. But he would meditate for hours over a text. And he would exercise his mind for the best way to apply the text until "it went through him like a bolt of lightning." After he preached, he wrote down his sermon outline.

Preachers such as Jerry Falwell who are blessed with a photographic memory find this method works well. Falwell, however, usually has a single sheet of paper with key words listed. Less gifted men think that their "gift of gab" is as good as a thoughtful exposition of God's Word. Some preachers actually think that this method is more spiritual than preaching from a prepared message. There are two very misused verses of Scripture at this point. Psalm 81:10b says, "Open thy mouth wide, and I will fill it" (KJV). And Mark 13:11a says, "Take no thought beforehand what ye shall speak" (KJV). Careful interpretation of either text, however, will give no comfort to the lazy preacher who does not wish to toil terribly in the study. The euphoria of having everyone listening to you might be intoxicating, but God does not need a drunk in the pulpit.

As a rule, don't plan to preach this way, but be ready to do so. Live in the Word and in close fellowship with the Living Word. "Always be prepared to give an answer to everyone who asks you to give the reason for the hope that you have" (1 Peter 3:15b). But if you come to time for the sermon and don't have a message from heaven, admit it. Don't mount the pulpit and take thirty minutes to prove it.

One final appeal: Don't lock yourself into only one delivery option.

Try others and try them more than once. You will find the one that fits your gifts best, but a variety in delivery might be as helpful as variety in homiletical plans. And there will be occasions when your preferred form of delivery will not meet the need.

This has been a long chapter, but it is barely a thumbnail sketch of homiletics. We will now turn to one special kind of sermon that a pastor would do well to master. Some people call it life-situation preaching. Other people call it pastoral preaching. We will consider it under the title "problem-solving preaching."

chapter five

PROBLEM-SOLVING PREACHING

A STUDENT CAME ONE DAY TO Fred Craddock's advanced Greek reading class in tennis togs. When the professor called on him to read and parse a difficult passage, he did so expertly. At the end of class, Professor Craddock stopped him and asked, "What did you think about Paul's statement: 'I could wish myself accursed for my brethren, my kinsmen according to the flesh'?"

The student answered, "Very unprofessional."

"What?" asked the puzzled professor.

"Very unprofessional," repeated the student, explaining, "A minister should never become so personally involved with the problems of people. See ya, Prof." And with that, he was off to tennis.

Should a shepherd get involved with the problems of the sheep? Only if he cares about them. In this chapter we will consider the following questions: What is problem-solving preaching? How does a preacher prepare this kind of pastoral sermon? What are some benefits of this approach? What hazards must we avoid?

WHAT IS PROBLEM-SOLVING PREACHING?

Problem-solving preaching is a pastor's pulpit ministry to his own flock, offering the Word of God to meet their specific needs. It is a shepherd's bringing the encouraging Word to his struggling sheep. I suppose that a visiting preacher might also address the needs of another shepherd's flock. But if he does so successfully, he is doing pastoral preaching. Walter Brueggeman's phrase "preaching to the baptized" led to William Willimon's book by that title. A chaplain might make a good pastoral preacher, although perhaps the term "life-situation preaching" would seem more fitting. An evangelist might master this form, but it is more likely that the shepherd who knows the sheep will be best able to feed them and guide them.

C. H. Dodd, in one small book, made quite a large impact on preaching theory. In *The Apostolic Preaching and Its Development*, Dodd distinguished between two kinds of preaching in the early New Testament church. Using two Greek words, Dodd distinguished between *kerygma* and *didache*. *Kerygma* was the gospel preached to the lost to evangelize them. *Didache* was ethical instruction to the saved to edify them. The two kinds of apostolic preaching had separate target audiences—the lost and the saved, respectively. Each had a distinct aim, to evangelize or to edify. The nature of the proclamation of each was distinct. The *kerygma* was gospel proclamation. The *didache* was ethical instruction.[1]

Jesus did both evangelistic preaching and pastoral preaching. Matthew records both kinds in one passage: "Jesus went through all the towns and villages, teaching in their synagogues, preaching the good news of the kingdom . . ." (Matt. 9:35). On this evangelizing tour, Jesus was moved with compassion for the multitudes. He saw them as "harassed and helpless, like sheep without a shepherd" (v. 36b). Then follows a message to His disciples that defines the need: "The harvest is plentiful but the workers are few" (v. 37). It calls for prayer as the way to meet that need: "Ask the Lord of the harvest, therefore, to send out workers into his harvest field" (v. 38).

Some people argue that every sermon should focus on a single problem and seek to bring the Word of God to bear on that problem. If that is so, a legitimate need for a specific pastoral focus still exists.

HOW DOES THE PASTOR PREPARE THIS KIND OF SERMON?

The procedure for preparing this message differs from the method for building any sermon only in a few particulars.

1. *The sermon preparation starts where the flint of human hurt strikes a spark on the steel of divine revelation.* The sermon might begin as a seed thought while the pastor is reading the Bible devotionally. Or it might come in more concentrated Bible study. Because the pastor knows his people, he recognizes that this text speaks to a specific problem and could help some of his flock.

At other times, the pastor sees the need before a specific text comes to his attention. In this case, the sermon cannot begin in earnest until a text comes forth to speak to that need. The pastor might go to the Word in search of God's solution. When the need comes to mind before the text, the preacher must take extra care. The temptation will be to develop the sermon topically, skipping all over the Bible for proof texts to prop up the preacher's own ideas. Such a sermon is less likely to be a true biblical sermon.

2. *Study proceeds on both tracks. Exegete the text faithfully, and analyze the problem carefully.* One track is the problem; the other track is the solution. The problem is always some human hurt—guilt, sorrow, doubt, fear, disappointment, or a hundred other struggles of mortals. The solution always comes from the Bible. Otherwise, it is not a real sermon but just the opinion of the speaker. It might be a religious opinion, and even a well-informed opinion, but if it is not drawn from accurate interpretation and application of God's Word, it is not a sermon.

3. *State the problem with clarity and candor.* This is a crucial step. It is important that the preacher not introduce a straw man that he can easily demolish. If the pastor does not present the problem fairly, no one will see it as a true personal issue. Christians do have real

problems, and unless they have become too jaded by repeated disappointment from the pulpit, they come to church looking for genuine solutions. Let the preacher be fair, honest, and as objective as possible in stating the problem. He should avoid making a judgment about the problem from the first. Suppose he is dealing with fear, worry, or indifference. He might be tempted to label the problem a sin from the start. That will not help his listeners identify with the problem. Unless they can see it as *their* problem, they will not find the sermon very helpful.

In the first two minutes of a life-situation sermon, many people in the congregation should be saying to themselves, *Now the pastor is talking about something I need to hear. This is a problem in my life, and I would welcome a solution.*

So, the problem-solving sermon starts with a real problem in the lives of the real people who sit before the preacher. Then the whole sermon moves toward a biblical solution to that problem. If it is skillfully crafted, such a sermon will have the listener thinking at first, *That is a knotty problem. How will the preacher ever untie it?* And, at the end, the listener will be delighted that God's Word did indeed have the answer.

4. *Structure the message.* As in the preparation of any sermon, the preacher must gather illustrations and other supporting materials. True-to-life examples are essential to problem-solving sermons. They help the listeners conceptualize the problem and visualize the solution. As in all sermon preparation, an incubation period helps the planning process. These steps may move in tandem with the process of structuring the sermon.

The structure may be as simple as the following two divisions. The first division is a statement of the problem, and the second division is the scriptural solution. Another plan for problem solving is sometimes called "the chase technique." It also begins with the definition of the problem. The sermon then progresses by exploring in order several inadequate solutions. Finally, it offers the biblical text as the right solution.

Suppose, for example, that the problem is doubt. In the space of one week, three or four people approached me with their own uncertainty about spiritual reality. A young man in jail asked me, "How do you know if there really is a God or if the Bible is true?" Another person asked sincerely, "How can I be sure which religion is right?" Then a woman who was decorating for our church banquet said, "I want to know something. Do preachers really believe everything they preach? Sometimes I wonder." These were not agnostics looking for a debate. Each person was a sincere searcher who was struggling to displace doubt with assurance.

The sermon that grew out of those conversations described those case studies briefly in the introduction. Then I presented the text. I chose John 7:17, where Jesus dealt with doubters. He said, "Whoever is willing to do what God wants will know whether what I teach comes from God or whether I speak on my own authority" (TEV). The development drew on scriptural case studies. The first division stated, Don't despair of doubt. Face it and admit it. Abraham, Elijah, John the Baptist, and Peter all showed that doubt is a common human problem. I testified, also, of a time in my own experience when doubt greatly disrupted my Christian pilgrimage.

In the second sermon division, I balanced that by emphasizing that doubt is not to be encouraged or celebrated. Doubt might be the friend of scientific investigation, but we do not enter into spiritual reality through that door. There is no premium on doubt in the Word of God.

Then the third division came to the thesis of the sermon: We conquer doubt by willing obedience to the Word of God. Here I developed the text. Sometimes it works better to save the text until the solution stage in the sermon. Those who listen through traditional ears might think that the preacher has a very long introduction and a very brief body of the sermon.

A PROBLEM-SOLVING SERMON STRUCTURE

I. A serious problem needs to be fixed.
II. What shall we do?
   Solution A will not work.

Solution B is inadequate.
Solution C is also no solution at all.

III. Solution X is God's answer to the problem.
It is practical.
It is desirable.
It is what we need to fix the problem.

A master of this approach to pastoral preaching was Harry Emerson Fosdick. When I was a college student and a young seminarian, I was troubled by my teachers' use of Fosdick as a model. I knew that he called himself a "Modernist" and held a view of Scripture that I found offensive. But as I made homiletics the major focus of my studies, I developed an appreciation for his method. His sermons were models of rhetorical structure. I also discovered one thing that seemed ironic: This pastor with a liberal view of Scripture was more faithful to anchor his sermon in a text than many of the people who criticized him. In addition, his mastery of sermon style made him worth studying. Fosdick preached one sermon on the radio, and a desperately bereaved young pastor thought, *That man could help me.* He went to New York City, where Fosdick was serving Riverside Church, and got an appointment with the pastor. When he left the pastor's study, he said softly to the secretary, "He put all the stars back into my sky."

WHAT ARE SOME HAZARDS TO THIS APPROACH?

It will be wise for the pastor to see not only the value of problem-solving preaching but also some traps along the way.

1. *It is tempting for the preacher to substitute psychology for true biblical exposition.* The pastor who has a little academic training in psychology should especially beware this trap. The way to avoid substituting pop psychology for the truth of God is to ensure that everything you say from the pulpit has "Thus saith the Lord" stamped on it. I do not mean to decide what you want to say and then search for a proof text. Remember the McDill Rule: "Let the text shape the sermon."

2. If a pastor does attack a real problem, he had better have a real solution. If the pastor does not have an answer from God's Word, he had better not air the problem. It is possible to do a better job of defining the problem than showing the solution. This is one reason it works better to discover the biblical truth and then match it to the life situation. The preacher must be a constant student of the Bible. Reading it through repeatedly will pay great reward. It will bless and enrich the reader, and it will be an unfailing fountain of refreshment for the hungry sheep who expect to be fed. Whatever the human problem—depression, failure, fear, or whatever—the Bible has the answer.

3. There is a danger that one might focus on problems that no one had before the preacher suggested it. In one pastorate, I reached a point close to what some have called "burnout." It is a problem among those in the helping professions. While looking for help for myself, I preached a sermon on burnout. Never again! In the next few weeks, I had any number of church workers saying, "That's my problem; I'm just burned out. I need to resign my class, my committee, my church duties."

4. The risk of betraying a confidence is a genuine hazard. It might be an example that the preacher uses. Listeners recognize themselves in a case study the pastor uses. Then they think that everyone in the congregation will also recognize them. Even to raise the fear that you might reveal a secret will hurt your chances of privately helping some other wounded soul.

5. A preacher must guard against pandering to felt needs at the cost of neglecting unrecognized needs. Some ministers, said Fosdick, might be so anxious to deal with felt needs in the congregation that they forget to arouse the consciousness of needs that are unfelt but real. The minister, he said, must not let his preaching be "narrowed to the conscious needs of mediocre people." They have some needs that they prefer not to face. Most of us would not choose to hear sermons on troubling ethical and social issues such as world hunger, race relations, or forgiving those who have hurt us.

6. It is tempting for some preachers to become wholly preoccupied with the issues of the hour. They think that because their sermon is stuffed with information from their reading in daily newspapers and magazines or from their viewing of this and that television documentary they are being relevant. Their sermons come out sounding more like an editorial with slight religious seasoning. In problem-solving preaching, however, the point of departure should be a vital issue to the listener. Then it is the preacher's business to bring the light of God's Word into those deep shadows. It is not for us to darken God's counsel with words without knowledge (Job 38:2). Jesus started with people where they were, but He made it His business to get to the core of the problem and move them on to where they ought to be. That is life-situation preaching, or what we are calling problem-solving preaching.

7. *The pastor must not think that this is the only way to do pastoral preaching.* The church needs to hear the great doctrines of the faith such as grace, mercy, holiness, the Atonement, and the sovereignty of God. They need sermons that lift them to God in praise and adoration and sermons that lead them to pray and teach them how. They need sermons that guide them to Christian positions on great ethical issues of our culture such as abortion, gambling, and race. A pastor will need to preach on matters of Christian stewardship of time and money and all of life. And even those who long ago anchored their soul in the Savior need to hear the gospel story again and again. This, too, may be considered pastoral preaching.

WHAT ARE SOME BENEFITS OF THIS APPROACH?

In spite of these hazards for the pastoral preacher, the blessings of learning to do it well are significant.

1. *It helps people.* This approach is called problem-solving preaching for good reason. Done well, it does guide a pilgrim people through personal problems, family problems, and societal problems. What pastor does not long to see his people overcome weakness and rise to victorious living? When Jesus saw the crowds, "he had compassion on them, because they were harassed and helpless, like sheep without a shepherd" (see Matt. 9:36). When we weep over our church members as Christ wept over Jerusalem, we are on the way to helping them.

2. *It is good for people to see that their pastor understands their struggles*

and cares. Sometimes a listener will be moved to come for a private conference with a pastor who seems to be in touch with personal problems. The sermon might not have dealt with that soul's burden at all, but it was a true problem-solving sermon. He will think, *My pastor has an understanding heart. I believe he would understand my problem.*

3. *In some larger churches, this might be the only way a pastor will ever counsel some of his people.* There are just not enough hours in the day for any pastor to fulfill all of the demands and duties that are placed on him. As the flock increases, it seems time for one-on-one counseling decreases. Some pastors decide that they will not do certain kinds of counseling—marital counseling, for example. Others try to expand the staff by hiring a specialist in counseling. Surely the man with the shepherd's heart will want to keep the personal touch. Pastoral preaching is one way to do so. Fosdick believed that the worth of a sermon could be measured by how many people asked for a private interview afterward.[2]

SOME MODELS OF PROBLEM-SOLVING PREACHING

F. W. Robertson

F. W. Robertson grew up in a military family on a military post and wanted a military career. His father, however, urged him toward the ministry. Shortly after he entered Oxford at age twenty-nine, an offer of an officer's commission came to him. But he had made his choice and did not turn back.

Robertson was thirty-two when he was ordained into the Anglican ministry and began what was to be an all-too-brief career. He spent his health in unrelenting toil. He would rise early, skip breakfast, and spend all morning in Bible study. Afternoons found him rushing from hovel to hovel in the slums with an intense schedule of ministry to London's misery. Evenings were for discussions with his rector. No exercise, no social life, no leisure did he allow himself until his health broke.

His doctor sent him to Switzerland for rest in 1846. When he came back the next year, he thought that he was ready for his own pastorate and began preaching at Trinity Chapel, Brighton. He was thoroughly evangelical in his theology and made his primary concern "the saving of souls." Nevertheless, other Low Church Anglicans were suspicious of his concern for social reform. It was a time of great change in England with social upheaval and theological tension. While Robertson was ministering in the slums of London, Karl Marx was in that city's library writing his *Communist Manifesto*.

Robertson took his sermon subject from the text, as did Alexander Maclaren and Charles Spurgeon. He is famous for his two-point sermons. He did not follow the inductive model of more recent "life-situation preachers." His sermon on "The Loneliness of Christ" takes John 16:31–32 as its text: "Behold, the hour cometh, yea is now come, that ye shall be scattered . . . and shall leave me alone: and yet I am not alone, because the Father is with me" (v. 32 KJV). It is, of course, a sermon about our struggle with loneliness too. The two sermon divisions were as follows:

I. The loneliness of Christ
II. The spirit or temper of that solitude[3]

He preached extemporaneously and wrote out his manuscript only on Sunday night after he had preached. After only six years at Brighton, his health broke again. At thirty-seven years of age, the brilliant mind that had memorized the whole New Testament in English and much of it in Greek was extinguished. He died thinking himself a failure. Only later were his sermons published. They are still read and widely praised.

Harry Emerson Fosdick

I have already mentioned Harry Emerson Fosdick. Born near Buffalo, New York, and educated at Colgate, Columbia, and Union Seminary, New York, he served as pastor of the Riverside Church for twenty years. His 1928 *Harper's* magazine essay "What Is the Matter with

Preaching?" set forth his method. The trouble with mediocre sermons is that they have no connection with life. Every sermon should have for its main business the solving of some problem. That is a sermon's only justifiable aim. Preaching is creative. It brings about in the lives of the congregation the thing about which it deals. "The real sermon must do more than discuss joy—it must produce it."

An example of Fosdick's art is the sermon titled "Handling Life's Second Best," suggested by Paul's experience in Acts 16 of "wanting Bithynia and getting Troas." Fosdick established the theme in the first five lines of the sermon:

> We are concerned today about a factual personal problem so nearly universal in its application that we need not be bothered by its exceptions: namely, that very few persons have a chance to live their lives on the basis of their first choice. We all live upon the basis of our second and third choices.[4]

Fosdick saw his sermon forms in three types: the box sermon, the tree sermon, and the river sermon. It is not always easy to categorize them as you read them. *The box sermon* is traditional rhetorical structure: first, second, third. The divisions of *the tree sermon* grow out of the "big truth" as branches grow out of the trunk. Fosdick considered his best type *the river sermon*. The message sweeps along between the banks without sharp distinction as to the various parts. This was also the hardest to do and the least often done.

George W. Truett

George W. Truett wanted to be a lawyer, but through the insistence of his home church, he determined that God's will for his life was to be a preacher. Before he entered Baylor, he successfully raised funds to save the school. Soon after he graduated, he was elected Baylor's president. He declined, however, saying that God had given him the shepherd heart.

Most of Truett's sermons expounded a brief text of Scripture in its context. Scores of them are still in print. Scan the titles and you will see the pastor's heart in sermons on "Christ and Human Suffering," "Need for Encouragement," "A Young Man and His Perils," "Life's Middle Time," and "Why Be Discouraged?" A sermon on "The Conquest of Fear" is based on Revelation 1:17b–18: "Fear not; I am the first and the last: I am he that liveth, and was dead; and, behold, I am alive for evermore, Amen; and have the keys of hell and of death" (KJV). The outline is simple. Jesus bids us—

I. Do not be afraid of life: "I am he that liveth"
II. Do not be afraid of death: ". . . and was dead"
III. Do not be afraid of eternity: ". . . and behold, I am alive forevermore."[5]

There is more to being a pastor than preaching, however, so we must leave this chapter and turn our attention to the pastor as a leader.

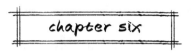

PASTORAL LEADERSHIP

I WAS SITTING IN THE DESERT SAUNA at Fitness World. I did not know the man sitting beside me by name, but somehow the conversation came around to churches. He asked me where I attended, and I said "Shreve City."

"Who's the pastor there?" he asked.

Now I should have said, "I'm the pastor," but I didn't. I said, "A fellow named Tucker."

"Oh yes," he said. "He used to be interim pastor at Brookwood when we were members there."

He was right about that. I couldn't resist the impulse to see where this would go next, so I ventured to ask, "Did he do a good job?"

"Oh yes," he said. "He's a good preacher." I'm sure that made me grin. I was just about ready to stick out my hand and introduce myself, but before I could accept the compliment, he added, "He's not much of a leader though. I think he just did what they wanted done."

ARE YOU A LEADER?

We might define pastoral leadership as the ability to influence a church to move together toward a common goal. But such a definition must allow for the fact that people do not always follow a faithful leader. It is often said, "You might think that you are a leader, but if you look around and no one is following, you are not a leader." By this standard, Jesus failed as a leader. There was a time in the ministry of Christ when the crowds fanatically followed Him. But crowds are fickle. "Many of his disciples turned back and no longer followed him" (John 6:66). There is pathos in His question to the twelve: "You do not want to leave too, do you?" (v. 67) Did Jesus suddenly cease to be a leader?

It was a short distance between the shouts of "Hosanna" on Palm Sunday and the shouts of "Crucify him!" four days later (Mark 11:9; 15:13). No doubt some of the same people were in both crowds. The sentiment of a church also can shift that dramatically. A pastor, therefore, should not be too hard on himself if he glances back at his followers and finds that they have turned into a mob chasing him. Nor should he be too proud of himself if he seems to enjoy an extended "honeymoon" of popularity.[1]

LEADERSHIP STYLES

If the church were a football game, there would be three models of leadership: coach, cheerleader, and quarterback. The coach does not get in the game although he might make all of the decisions from the sidelines. The coach trains the players, sets the game plan, and decides who gets in the game and when. Some coaches send every play into the huddle. The coach is the expert. Some pastors try to lead a church by the coach model.

Other pastors adopt the cheerleader model. Cheerleaders do not get into the game either. Nor do they decide strategy or implement it. Cheerleaders whip up support for whatever play the team runs. The decisions are made by someone else. This pastor is a promoter. Building morale is his thing. He is strong on encouragement and celebrating the success of those who do the work, but he works from the sidelines.

The pastor who ministers by the quarterback model leads as a participant. He is not a one-man show. Without every member of the team doing his or her part, the quarterback will fail and so will the team. He coordinates, encourages, and calls plays. He takes his lumps, along with the linemen and everyone else.

At different times, a pastor might need to be a coach, a cheerleader, or a quarterback. Perhaps in this football analogy, the player-coach combination more nearly fits the biblical model of a pastor. Like a coach, he has the task of equipping the saints to do the work of the ministry, but the pastor is a minister too. A leader has some responsibility for guiding the goal setting of the group. That pastor is no leader who gauges the sentiment of a church and then gets around in front (if I may change the metaphor a bit) like a little boy stepping out in front of a marching band. The parade moves on down Main Street, and he enjoys pretending that he is the drum major. Real leadership involves showing people when they are moving in the wrong direction. It means guiding them in the right path. Paul could say, "Follow my example, as I follow the example of Christ" (1 Cor. 11:1). Let it be the pastor's goal to do and say the same.

Everyone likes a winner. But in a football game, only one team can come out on top. The church must function in this kind of success-driven culture. Pressure builds on a pastor to get the numbers up. He is considered a loser if he cannot have better numbers this year than the church had last year. And he might regard himself as a failure if his church is not doing at least as well as the neighboring church. Indeed, as we have noted, some people say that only the leader of the winning team is a true leader.

THE CORPORATE LEADER STYLE

Some pastors take their model of leadership from the world of business or industrial management. Plenty of books are available about this style. And they do sell well to church leaders. The pastor becomes the chief executive officer at the head of a corporation. He is selling a service, competing with other churches for customers, clients, or prospects. Surveys tell him what the public wants in a church. His task, then, is to convince the public that his church can best fill that need. Slick advertising and public relations works for the corporation; it will work for the church as well. Do people want a church to educate their children, entertain their youth, and socialize everyone? Do they want excitement in the Sunday service and a warm, fuzzy feeling to take home? Well, let's get geared up to satisfy whatever the seekers are seeking this year. It's a matter of marketing the church.[2]

While Moses was on Mount Sinai, Aaron provided this kind of leadership for the new nation on a pilgrimage. They decided that they wanted gods that they could see. Aaron became a facilitator. He arranged for a great gathering of gold jewelry and ornaments. He supervised the casting and carving of a bull calf. That was their god. Aaron built an altar and declared a festival for the next day. On the morrow, they started early with sacrifices and burnt offerings to the idol. "Afterward they sat down to eat and drink and got up to indulge in revelry" (Exod. 32:6). So much for democratic devotion.

When Moses came down from the mountaintop, he saw the wild orgy of idolatry. He did not take a vote to determine his course of action. Moses was a leader, not a lackey. You might find that your church wants their pastor to be like Aaron. May God give you grace to be a man of God. Jesus makes a better model of a church leader because He is our pattern in all things. To that model we now turn.

LEARNING TO LEAD FROM JESUS

1. Jesus took the initiative. The leader casts the vision. Following Jesus, the pastor will aim to do not his own will but the will of the Father (John 5:30; 6:38). What that means in any given church setting is a matter to be determined in earnest prayer. When the leader is clear on the direction that God's Holy Spirit is pointing, he has the task of conveying that vision to those who follow. Here is one source of church strife: The pastor has one vision for the church, but various cliques have their own separate visions. One group, perhaps a senior adult department, sees their church as guardians of the traditions. Others, perhaps young couples, want to downplay tradition in the interest of reaching new people. The pastor's duty is to shape these and other interest groups into one dynamic church. Such blending is not an easy task.

2. *Jesus selected and enlisted helpers and trained them for their task.* See Him walking by the Sea of Galilee and saying to some people He had encountered earlier, "'Come, follow me,' Jesus said, 'and I will make you fishers of men'" (Matt. 4:19). The training was close and personal. A pastor who wants his members to become soul winners will take one with him and go soul winning. At first, the pastor does the evangelizing while his partner prays and watches. When that one learns how to do it, each can take another person to train. Jesus organized His men into teams. There were the Twelve who followed Him as disciples (pupils) and went where He sent them. Sometimes He sent them in teams of two. One time, He sent out thirty-five teams of two.

They learned to do by doing. When I was growing up, I often heard my mother introduce a correction to my behavior with "I've told you a thousand times this or that." For example, as a typical eight- or ten-year-old boy, I would usually hit the back screen door on the run. About the time I got to the bottom of the steps, I would hear, "Don't slam the door!" By then it was too late. The coil spring already had the screen door headed for another slam. But one day, Mother called me back and said, "I want you to go to the back door and open it and close it one hundred times without slamming it." That day, finally, I learned how to close the door. Somewhere along the way, I learned that merely telling is not teaching.

3. *Christ enabled His followers with delegated authority.* Like Christ, all of the pastor's work will be done at the Spirit's direction and in the power of the Holy Spirit. In the synagogue of Nazareth at the beginning of His ministry, Christ read a passage from Isaiah as the keynote for His ministry: "The Spirit of the Sovereign LORD is on me, because the LORD has anointed me to preach good news" (Isa. 61:1; cf. Luke 4:21). The people were amazed at the teaching of Jesus. They marveled, not only at its content but also at His manner of teaching. He did not teach as the scribes, *quoting* authority; He taught as one *having* authority (see Matt. 7:28; Mark 1:22; 3:11).

But a leader is also one who enables others. Christ called attention to the source of power for ministry as He commissioned His own to go in His name and continue His saving work: "All authority in heaven and on earth has been given to me. Therefore go and make disciples of all nations" (Matt. 28:18–19).

George Barna contrasted the leadership styles of U.S. presidents Jimmy Carter and Ronald Reagan. Carter was involved at all levels of decision making and became overwhelmed with the operational minutiae of a vast government bureaucracy. Carter's administration succeeded in relatively little of the agenda that he brought to the White House. Reagan had just as much bureaucracy but a different leadership style. Indeed, he was criticized for not being more involved with micromanagement. But Reagan focused on the big picture and left the details to his lieutenants. A leader is one who enables others.[3]

4. *Jesus modeled ministry for His disciples.* Jesus was not an ivory-tower leader. Watch Him in the Gospels, touching the untouchable leper, inviting Himself to dine with the despised publican, sitting on a dusty well curb offering water of life to a woman with a sordid life story. His disciples took note. Recall the object lesson of the night of His betrayal. In the Upper Room, He wrapped a towel about Himself in the manner of a lowly servant. Then He washed the feet of each disciple. He told them that He was giving them an example to follow.

Parents learn that children need both the model and the message. If a mother or a father only models service, the child learns that the role of the parent is to serve; the role of the child is to be served. But the wise parent will frequently remind the children, "In our family, we all serve each other." A pastor who mows the church lawn, weeds the flower beds, and trims the shrubbery is not necessarily setting a good example. He might be setting a bad precedent for the next pastor. But if he does these acts of humble service *and* calls others to help him, he is leading by example.

5. *Jesus accepted ultimate responsibility for failure or success.* In the case of Jesus, there could be no ultimate failure. The Cross, by divine providence, was no defeat for Christ. He could say, "On this rock I will build my church, and the gates of Hades will not overcome it" (Matt. 16:18). We mere mortals may succeed or fail. When we miss divine direction, we will fail. We will likewise fail when we try to do His work

in our human strength. The mark of a leader is that he takes responsibility for his failure. A wise pastor will learn from his mistakes.

LEADING PUBLIC WORSHIP

The first business of the church is worship. Out of worship flows evangelism, missions, education, and everything else the church does. Meaningful worship requires prayerful and thoughtful planning. Who is responsible for this planning?

1. *It is the pastor's duty to lead the church in worship.* Some pastors focus on their role as preacher and leave the leadership of worship to a musician. We should welcome the trend in evangelical churches for the pastor to return to his role as worship leader. Let's assume that the pastor is committed to the priority of worship and truly believes that, as the *Westminster Shorter Catechism* relates, the chief end of man "is to glorify God and to enjoy Him forever." How will he lead his congregation into a true experience of worship? This leadership begins with planning.

2. *Plan for worshipful music.* Because music is such a large part of evangelical worship tradition, a wise pastor will work with the church musicians. They will nearly always welcome the pastor's guidance in choice of a theme to focus the worship. I have a pastor friend who selects every hymn and the music for choir, soloists, organ, and piano from repertoires submitted to him. I know many pastors who leave the selection of music completely to the discretion of the music leader, without as much as a hint of what Scripture the pastor will use. I've been a guest preacher in churches where the song leader picked a few hymns during the piano prelude. Perhaps somewhere between those extremes is better planning.

3. *Involve the worshipers in leading worship.* Planning allows more active participation of laity in worship. A teenager, if carefully prepared, might do a great job of Scripture reading. And sometimes even a child can lead. The wise pastor will bless them and bless his church with this participation. The church where our family worships recently began using families to welcome guests. The father might begin with

a brief testimony of how this church led them to Christ and welcomed them into fellowship. The mother then explains how we register guests. Children who are old enough also have a part. This brief feature ends with the presentation of our pastor. Such things require planning.

4. *You can have freshness and vitality in worship without shocking the traditionalists.* A church does not have to follow a high-church liturgy to have high-quality worship. Nor is unstructured spontaneity a sign of being Spirit led. If you think that your church does not have a fixed ritual, just try changing a few things. Suppose that you placed the sermon first and the singing afterward. How would the church welcome that change? In one church, I moved the announcement time from early in the service to the end. We needed more time for counselors to deal adequately with those who responded to the invitation. Some longtime members treated that innovation as heresy. They wanted to get back in their comfortable rut. I'm sure that after I left, they soon did so.

LEADING BUSINESS MEETINGS

In some church traditions, an elder or church officer other than the pastor will moderate a church conference. In most churches, however, the pastor serves in this capacity. In any case, some things will help ensure that all things are done "in a fitting and orderly way" (1 Cor. 14:40).

1. *Prepare an agenda that everyone can follow.* The moderator calls the meeting to order. In church, why not do that with a Scripture reading and prayer? Something such as Romans 12:5 is appropriate: "So in Christ we who are many form one body, and each member belongs to all the others." If the minutes of the previous meeting are printed and distributed, draw attention to them and approve them, noting any corrections. The treasurer's report and reports of other boards and committees follow. Unfinished business comes next, followed by new business. Announcements may be made before adjournment.

2. *Follow good rules of order without slavish legalism.* Your church constitution or bylaws might specify *Robert's Rules of Order*. It would

be well to get acquainted with those rules, but in most cases you will not want to follow them slavishly. For example, someone will get weary of the discussion and call out "Question!" as if that automatically stops all discussion. Usually, they don't even wait to be recognized. Properly, to "move the previous question" is a request that the debate end and the question under discussion be decided by vote. Technically, the moderator should first put to the body the decision to end debate. Then, if that passes by two-thirds of the vote, the "previous question" is put to a vote without further discussion. It might be better, however, for the moderator to encourage the discussion to continue as long as lively exchange is occurring and moving toward consensus. Then, when the assembly is ready to vote, there will be no need for a motion to end debate. One vote will do.

Of course, the larger a church gets, the less likely it is to function in the simple town-meeting tradition. In today's megachurch, the staff takes responsibility and makes many decisions on behalf of the congregation. This delegated authority is necessary for the church to work efficiently. I once was in a church conference in which the whole assembly took up the question of what to serve in the church nursery: cookies and punch or crackers and milk? How much time should be budgeted for a discussion of this sort? Even in a small church, most members would be happy for such a decision to be handled administratively.

At the other extreme, I was also in Thomas Road Baptist Church in Lynchburg, Virginia, one Sunday when pastor Jerry Falwell came to the pulpit with a document in his hand. As I recall that day in 1978, this is about the way the business meeting went.

The pastor said, "As you know, we have decided to buy Candlers Mountain and relocate the college there. Our lawyer tells us that since we are a Baptist church, we have to vote to do that. He's prepared the papers, and I have them here if anyone wants to see them. Is there any discussion?" Two thousand members had not one question or comment. "All in favor, say 'Aye.'" A great chorus of "Aye" gave the church's blessing to a multimillion-dollar transaction. Meeting adjourned. With hardly a sixty-second detour, we went on with worship.

A reporter interviewed Pastor Falwell's administrative assistant in those days and asked about an earlier financial crisis that had been widely reported. He asked if that could have happened in the typical Southern Baptist church. The answer was, "Probably not, but then we probably would be a church of a few hundred members instead of thousands." Thomas Road at that time was affiliated only with Baptist Bible Fellowship. "Our churches are typically pastor-led," he said. "Southern Baptists tend to be lay-led." It is a valid generalization.

3. *Christian courtesy and fairness should govern all.* The moderator can set a tone that will encourage the majority to respect the opinions of the minority. Christian unity is crucial. Sometimes in a democratic decision strong feelings will exist on different sides of the issue. Most people will accept the decision of the body if they sense that the church gave everyone a hearing.

4. *Encourage the church to think of themselves as the body of Christ.* We seek not our own will but the mind of Christ, our Head. A church is not an ordinary democracy ruled by the people; it is a spiritual democracy seeking the mind of Christ. Understanding that fact will make a difference in the way we do business—or, better put, *the way we do ministry.*

In my seminary days, I served as the pastor of a church in which the local banker was the church treasurer. He read the monthly financial statement, and I cringed each time he came to the bottom line: "The church this month had a *net profit* (or a *net loss*) of so many dollars."

ORGANIZING FOR MINISTRY

How much organization does a church need? A small church does not need as much organization as a larger one, but nearly every church will need certain officers and committees to carry out its mission. In addition to the pastor, it should have deacons (or elders, or stewards in some churches). The church will need a clerk to keep official records, a treasurer to keep financial records, and trustees to represent the church in legal matters such as signing deeds and other documents.

Committees might be as many or as few as the need requires. Some permanent committees will function year-round. Temporary committees may do their work and be dismissed. The permanent committees might include ushers, baptism, Lord's Supper, finance, nominating, personnel, music, and library committees. Some churches have a membership committee. Some have an evangelism committee. Still others try to avoid compartmentalizing evangelism in the hope that it will permeate the work of every committee.

Temporary committees, for example, the budget planners, do their work seasonally. Unless they also serve as a finance committee to administer the budget, their work ends when the budget is adopted. A pulpit committee (or pastor search committee) functions in congregational government when the church is without a pastor. When the church has a building fund drive, it will need a capital giving committee, whatever it is called. If possible, this committee should be separate from the building committee.

As a church grows, the committee structure can grow and involve more people. The church staff should grow also. The first paid staff member after the pastor will be, in most cases, a secretary or a custodian. The first paid age-group worker will probably be a nursery worker because much of that work seems to be babysitting. Then the church might call a minister of music, minister of education, youth minister, or some combination of those functions. A talented servant might be willing to wear more than one hat. As a church expands, a need might arise for a paid business manager, church hostess, or assistant to the pastor.

In the next chapter, we consider one especially challenging administrative problem for the pastor: how to manage conflict in the church.

chapter seven

CONFLICT MANAGEMENT

CONFLICT IN THE CHURCH, OF COURSE, is not a modern phenomenon. Jesus spent much of His ministry facing the opposition of the religious establishment. That same establishment was the main source of trouble for the first-century church. Internal church conflict occurred as well. The Jerusalem Council in Acts 15, for example, struggled with a crucial theological issue: whether the church was going to be a branch of Judaism or a wholly new body, made up of Jews and Gentiles. As soon as that issue was settled, Paul and Barnabas, the prototype mission team, had a sharp disagreement over whether to give John Mark a second chance. They only agreed to disagree and to part company (Acts 15:39).

In writing to the Galatians, Paul recounts a major confrontation that he had with Peter. It was a matter of grave concern to Paul, the Apostle to the Gentiles, that Peter seemed rather two-faced. For a while, Peter could eat ham sandwiches with the Gentiles in good conscience. But then some traditional Jews came down from First Church at Jerusalem. Peter suddenly became kosher again and withdrew from Gentile fellowship.

Paul singled out Euodias and Syntyche in one of his letters and publicly urged them to be of one mind. The elder John thought it necessary to rebuke and warn Diotrophes, who loved to have preeminence and acted as the church boss. These instances only sample the dissension that arose in the early church.

THREE KINDS OF CONFLICT FOR THE PASTOR

Most of the conflict in a pastor's professional life is one of three kinds. The first type is the pastor's own inner conflicts. A second type is conflict between those who need the pastor to be peacemaker. Warring factions or individuals get out of fellowship with each other. The third type of conflict targets the pastor himself. From time to time, the pastor will find tension arising with another church member. It might be conflict with another staff member, a board member, or the board as a whole. The pastor might find himself on one side of a controversy when the whole church and the whole community seem to be on the other side. In the following sections, we consider in order each of these three kinds of conflict.

THE PASTOR'S OWN INNER CONFLICT

One study of ministerial stress identified eighty potential causes of stress. Some of them are common to any occupation, but some are particularly acute for pastors. The study identified about seven broad areas of inner stress for the minister in addition to conflicts between the minister and others.

1. *Time management.* The demands are too many, the hours too few. The pastor has to learn to make a daily "to-do" list. Ideally, you will work from a one-year list of goals, but you eat that elephant one bite at a time. Break it down into goals for this month, this week, and today. At the end of each workday, list the chores that you must do the next day. But don't lay it aside until you have gone one step further. Arrange the duties in order of priority. The next day, start with the item at the top of the list, and don't quit until you can mark it off as done. Then go to the second item. You might not get through all of your list today, but you will get the most important jobs done. And you will get much more done by staying focused. There is more that

needs to be said on this matter. I will deal with it further in chapter 14, "The Pastor's Stewardship of Time."

    2. Financial difficulties. The pastor's pay is usually not large considering the years of training that he must invest and the expectations imposed by church and community. Although some people think that the pastor has a big break on taxes with housing provided, they forget that he pays Social Security at the self-employed rate. The pastor might not have the same liberty to decide about his tithes and offerings as others do. Beggars call on the pastor. If the church does not provide him a benevolence fund, his own budget takes the hit. Financial struggle is a source of stress on the pastor and everyone in his family.

    3. Living up to everyone's expectations. It is a struggle to maintain a standard of living comparable to that in the church and the community when the pastor's salary is below average. Then other expectations cause additional pressure. The pastor's children are often expected to be paragons of virtue and examples of Christian decorum—even if they play with the deacon's kids. The pastor's wife might be pressured to serve in every volunteer role that the former pastor's wife filled.

    4. The minister's own feelings. People in the caring professions sometimes experience burnout. People with high standards might feel guilty for not measuring up to their own expectations. A pastor might think, *I don't witness enough. I'm not reaching my community. I don't see real change in lives of those to whom I preach.*

    5. Church administration. When pastors are asked to rank six areas of ministerial duties according to their ideal order of importance, they usually say that their first responsibility is preacher, then pastor, and then "priest" in the sense of performing certain sacred duties. The last three, in order of importance to the minister, are teacher, organizer, and administrator. When the same pastors, however, are asked to rank the same six functions by the time they actually spend on each, the last will become first. Most pastors spend the largest portion of their time as administrators, even though they consider that duty the least vital. Preaching and teaching get the least of his time although the ministry of the Word is certainly the top priority. This reality is a recipe for stress. Budgets, buildings, and committee meetings—who is sufficient for all of these things?[1]

6. Duty to family. The wife and children need and deserve a piece of the same man whom everyone else needs. The pastor, like everyone else, might have parents and grandparents who need some of his attention. Pastors are more likely to live far from their roots than are other family groups. The inner conflict kicks in the afterburners when the pastor decides to sacrifice these "personal problems" on the altar of a church-first priority system.

7. Issues of personal health. Who has time for exercise? How can I watch my diet with all of these "eating meetings"? Rest? Vacation? Forget it. Some of my ministerial brothers in college used to say, "I'd rather burn out than rust out." Either way, you are out.

THE SCRIPTURAL STANDARD FOR RESTORATION OF FELLOWSHIP

Two other areas of conflict are all too common in the church. But first, let us recall the teaching of Jesus that applies to broken fellowship in the church. What should a pastor do when the church harmony is broken? He should follow the clear guidelines of Jesus in Matthew 18:15–17.

> If your brother sins against you, go and show him his fault, just between the two of you. If he listens to you, you have won your brother over. But if he will not listen, take one or two others along, so that "every matter may be established by the testimony of two or three witnesses." If he refuses to listen to them, tell it to the church; and if he refuses to listen even to the church, treat him as you would a pagan or a tax collector.

A four-step process is involved here. The first step is to go to the offending brother one to one (v. 15). The goal is not exclusion but restoration. If the first step ends in restored fellowship, the harmony is back. There is no need to go further.

If the second step is needed, it is to involve one or two others who can help with the effort to restore (v. 16). They will encourage the offender to repent and enjoy forgiveness and restoration. Both parties might need to do some changing of mind, for rarely is the fault all on one side. The witnesses might be helpful counselors at this point. The goal is still to restore the fellowship of the church. But in case it needs to go further, these one or two others will be able to tell the church that this effort was made and was unsuccessful.

The third step, then, is "tell it to the church" (v. 17). This step is not the place to begin a matter but rather the place to end it. If the offender still will not hear the church, he is to be regarded as no longer a part of the body. Exclusion is the final resort. With that reminder, let's focus on the other two major areas of conflict.

THE PASTOR AS PEACEMAKER

When the fellowship of the church hits a sour note, the pastor must restore the harmony. Euodias and Syntyche are in every church. They are at odds with each other (cf. Phil. 4:2). Neither will even sit on the same side of the church as the other. Paul said, "Help these women" (v. 3a). Outside rivalries also exist, such as a church in conflict with its neighborhood or the city council over zoning issues. These conflicts, however, do not usually threaten the peace and spiritual prosperity of the fellowship. They can even draw a church together.

When the harmony is broken, what can the pastor do as peacemaker?

1. *A pastor might need to develop some skill at admonishing.* People who are out of fellowship must be reconciled for Jesus' sake. Take, for example, the case of a Diotrephes-type person who loves the preeminence and acts as the church boss. He can make a real stink if anyone fails to acknowledge his long and distinguished service. He has come to expect others in the church to yield to his leadership. This fellow will be hard to deal with simply because he probably does have a distinguished record of service in that church. Everyone knows it. Even those who don't appreciate his spirit would rather give in to his demand for deference than incur his disfavor. Some pastors adopt this expedient also.

2. *Some church members might need to be evangelized.* Sweeping a

fellowship problem under the rug does not solve it. John, the Elder, had a different approach. "I will call attention to what he is doing" (3 John 10a). He suggested that the brother might not be a brother at all. "Anyone who does what is evil has not seen God" (v. 11c).

3. *Other members might need patient nurture.* Not every case of conflict is a matter of an unsaved church member, of course. Paul dealt with a very carnal church at Corinth. They were spiritual infants and adolescents. They needed nourishing on the pure milk of God's Word so they could grow up.

4. *Apply the biblical standard in every case.* I've not seen a statistical survey of this point, but I would estimate that most of a pastor's counseling will involve family problems, and most of that will be husband-wife conflicts. This is the day of easy, no-fault divorce. Many of these cases will not come to the pastor's attention until the couple has already decided to end the marriage. When you do have an opportunity to offer counsel, start from the ideal set out by Christ: "What God has joined together, let man not separate" (Mark 10:9).

5. *The pastor must endeavor to restore the offender gently considering his own frailty.* My telephone rang about 2 A.M. A frantic young mother of several children needed me to come at once. She and her husband had been arguing. He threatened to kill her and himself. Then he took his pistol and walked off into the woods. I knew not to get into that triangle alone, but I didn't know who else to take with me at that hour but my wife. We had our first baby sleeping and couldn't leave him. So hurriedly dressing, the three of us drove the ten miles out to a rural house. I was aware that we were putting our very lives in jeopardy—not just mine but my wife's and our baby's as well. Eventually, I found the man out in the pitch darkness and talked him into giving me the pistol. We agreed to take the wife and children back to our house for the rest of the night. He promised to behave himself at his house.

One would think that, out of such sacrificial service, a family would develop undying gratitude to such a pastor and his wife. But another dynamic is at work here. As long as that pastor is in the same church and knows their darkest secrets, their conflict is not fully and finally resolved. I did not understand that fact in my early pastoral experience.

So it was a surprise to me when some of the opposition in the church began to organize against their pastor, and this young couple joined the opposition. In other churches in the years since, that story with variations has played itself out more. The pastor becomes something like the garbage man. He provides a vital service to the community, but we want him to take the garbage and go.

"A new broom sweeps clean," said a layman to his pastor, justifying a group agitating for a pastoral change. The pastor replied, "The truth is, the old broom knows where the dirt is." The rest of this chapter will deal with conflict that comes as opposition against the pastor.

WHEN THE PASTOR IS THE OCCASION OF CONFLICT

Some of the causes for opposition against the pastor might be legitimate. Is he working or playing most of the week? Some pastors do spend entirely too much time on the golf course or at some other hobby. A pastor might simply not be doing his job. If he is lazy, won't study, can't preach, and doesn't care to learn, people have a legitimate complaint. Sometimes moral issues or issues of doctrinal defection justify defrocking a cleric.

A leader needs the ability to get along with people. Most pastors are men and most men rate themselves highly on this skill. One psychological study by random sample of male adults asked the subjects to rank their leadership ability and several other skills. On the ability to get along with people, one man in four put himself in the very top 1 percent. Six in ten put themselves in the top 10 percent. And all subjects put themselves in the top half of the population. They were like Garrison Keillor's mythical Lake Wobegon "where all the children are above average." In the same survey, 70 percent rated themselves in the top 25 percent on leadership ability, and only 2 percent thought themselves below average. If that survey were given to pastors, I suppose as a group, we would exaggerate the findings even more.[2]

Other complaints are not so well grounded. Often, they are simply personality clashes or power struggles. They might never be resolved as long as both strong personalities work in the same church. In a large church, especially in a city where other churches are available, it is easier for the layman to move his membership than for the pastor to move his. But the layman might not see it that way. He might think of the pastor as a temporary sojourner. The layman's family might have been leaders in the church for three generations. Guess who will leave first?

A pastor usually has a better following while he is new than later. That period is often called "the honeymoon." But in some cases a new pastor will find resistance simply because he is new and has not yet earned the trust of the congregation. In *Dying for Change*, Leith Anderson told of going to be the pastor of a church when he was thirty-two years old. With nineteen years of pastoral experience, he was hardly a novice. In the first year, he tried to change the traditional order of service in one small detail. He placed the invocation *after* the first hymn instead of *before* as it had traditionally been in that church. But that was not a small matter to the congregation. The storm grew so fierce that he had to change it back. But in time he earned their trust so that eight years later they followed him to change both the name of the church and its location and to build a new building costing millions.[3]

We have suggested already that churches do not always follow the pastor's leadership. Especially in twenty-first-century democratic societies, people follow only those whom they choose to follow. And they might decide at any time to quit following. One pastor described his experience thus: "When they were recruiting me, they said, 'Pastor, you just come and tell us what to do, and we will do it. We need a leader. We are ready to follow.'

"That's what they *said*. But what they *did* was a different story. Oh, they followed me all right. But they followed like a pack of cur dogs follows a stranger through the community—barking and growling and nipping at his heels until he is quite gone!"

WHAT IS A PASTOR TO DO?

When the pastor is the target of criticism, what should he do?

1. *Be sure that you listen for any truth in the complaints.* When you are wrong, admit it. And even when you are right, don't jump to your

own defense. You might be standing on the moral high ground with the Word of God clearly backing you, but you have little to gain in defending yourself. Hopefully, others will do so. But if not, try to learn from your critics. And distinguish between defending your position and defending yourself.

2. Be sure that when you do take a stand it is on an issue that matters. Some issues are worth fighting over. Others are not. What color to paint the nursery is not worth a fuss. Whether church members should be born again matters. Plenty of issues will arise that are weighty. At times, a pastor will have to take a stand on very divisive issues. When such issues surface, we would hope that they are clear issues of Bible doctrine such as the authority of Scriptures, the deity of Christ, or the blood atonement. Unfortunately, in our day, these are not the issues that stir passion. More often, people are stirred by moral and social issues: divorce, race relations, poverty, capital punishment, war, abortion, homosexual rights, and prayer in public schools. For the pastor to be silent on the burning issues of the day is gross dereliction of duty. To expect that he will always win the whole church over to his understanding of the biblical position is dreaming.

3. Sometimes it is good to seek the help of an impartial mediator. Some denominational bodies are training mediators to help churches resolve major disputes. A mediator helps estranged parties clarify what they really consider important in the matter at issue. He might help those who are alienated move toward each other enough to get back together on common ground. If the issues are beyond resolution, a mediator can help negotiate a Christian parting of the ways. If you seek the help of a mediator, ensure that it is a mediator and not an arbitrator who is merely calling himself a mediator. "Blessed are the peacemakers, for they will be called sons of God" (Matt. 5:9).

In some church traditions, a bishop or other executive has the authority to move a pastor to a new field of service. After appropriate consultation, and often in concert with other church officials, he decides what is in the best interest of the church, the minister, and the cause of Christ. This can often be done without disruptive debate and placing blame. A Methodist superintendent in my community came to serve a district of some seventy-five churches. His goal was for pastors and churches to work together for long tenure. Before he retired a few years ago, almost every church had changed pastors at least once.

4. Don't be devastated to find that not everyone loves the pastor with undying love. Jesus said, "Blessed are you when men hate you, when they exclude you and insult you and reject your name as evil, because of the Son of Man. Rejoice in that day and leap for joy, because great is your reward in heaven. For that is how their fathers treated the prophets" (Luke 6:22–23).

When J. D. Grey was a fifteen-year-old boy, "Miss Ethel" was his Sunday school teacher. When he graduated from Union University in Jackson, Tennessee, in 1929, Miss Ethel gave him a Bible. In the flyleaf, she pinned the following words, which he showed to me some fifty years later when, as a young pastor, I visited J. D. Grey in his study at First Baptist Church, New Orleans, Louisiana:

> Men may misjudge thy aim,
> Think they have cause to blame,
> Say thou art wrong!
> Go on thy quiet way;
> God is thy Judge, not they.
> Fear not! Be strong!

Those words, which he had never seen anywhere else, became something of a life ambition for that pastor and civic leader, who was well acquainted with controversy.

PREACHING ON CONTROVERSIAL ISSUES

A pastor retired after more than forty years in the same church. A reporter interviewed him for a feature article and asked the secret of his long and happy tenure. He did not hesitate: "In forty years, I have never preached on a controversial subject." Personally, I would not want to be standing in that brother's sandals at the judgment seat of Christ.

He was in the pulpit through years of great turmoil. Did he have no word from the Lord throughout the civil rights movement? When people were making up their minds about the abortion issue, did he keep quiet? Did he never disturb the tranquility of his congregation with thoughts of world hunger? Or the spread of legalized gambling? Or the tyranny of alcohol and tobacco addiction? Did he have nothing to say about the flood of pornography in print, on television, and at the movies? I'm sure that he also kept quiet about sex education in public schools. That would certainly be controversial. And he wouldn't dare address the issue of prayer in public schools; good people are on both sides of that issue.

A belief is prevalent that preaching ought never to disturb. That belief does not come from the Bible. Humorist Finley Peter Dunne's "Mister Dooley" quipped that the function of a journalist is "to comfort the afflicted, and afflict the comfortable." The same can be said of a preacher. Stephen's preaching disturbed people. So did Paul's. So did John's. So did the preaching of Jesus. To be sure, they paid the consequences in stoning, imprisonment, beatings, exile, and the Cross. And those who have come after them have also paid for their fidelity to the Word. Sometimes their fate has been less violent but more subtle. Economic boycott, excommunication, malice and misunderstanding, threats and intimidation—these pressures are no less real than the more violent treatment. Nor is social ostracism necessarily more merciful than death.

The role of a prophet has never been easy. Jesus said, "Woe to you when all men speak well of you, for that is how their fathers treated the false prophets" (Luke 6:26). Following are some suggestions for the preacher whose calling requires him to deal with divisive issues in the pulpit.

1. Accept the fact that it is a part of your calling. You can't always preach smooth platitudes. You are commanded, "Preach the Word; be prepared in season and out of season; correct, rebuke and encourage— with great patience and careful instruction" (2 Tim. 4:2).

2. Be sure that you are delivering God's message. Some preachers are so taken with their own opinions that they assume that everyone else is dying to hear them as well. The question that the church is asking is the question that King Zedekiah asked Jeremiah: "Is there any word from the LORD?" (Jer. 37:17). May the pastor's answer ever be the answer of that prophet: "Yes." The pulpit is no place for an opinionated tyrant to give vent to his frustration. If they put you on a cross, let it be because you spoke God's truth, not because you were an obnoxious egoist.

3. Be sure that your spirit and attitude are right. Some preachers can preach on hell and give the impression that it would be a delight to see those seated before them burning there. We must speak the truth in love. When I was a college student in my first pastorate, I was told, "If you love your people, you can tell them anything they need to hear. If you don't, there are some things better left unsaid." That sounded good to me at the time. Since then, I've lived through a few rejections. Such platitudes once caused me to doubt my suitability for the role of pastor. Let me remind my young readers that Jesus also suffered rejection. They rejected the message and killed the Messenger. Do you think it was because He didn't love them enough?

The pastorate is not all warfare. It includes times of great joy as well as deep sorrow. In the next chapter, we turn to weddings and funerals. These two ministries, as different as they are, have much in common.

chapter eight

WEDDINGS AND FUNERALS

THE FIRST MIRACLE OF JESUS, AS John's gospel tells the story, was at a wedding. At that joyful celebration, He turned water into wine (John 2:1–11). The last miracle was at the grave of His friend Lazarus, where "Jesus wept" before He restored His friend to life (John 11:35). Every pastor who walks with his people will have his own mixture of joy and sorrow. In this chapter, we focus first on a pastor's opportunity to share the joy of weddings. Then we turn to the privilege of offering God's comforting grace in the tender times of sorrow.

TOUGH DECISIONS ABOUT WEDDINGS

In the matter of weddings, a pastor must face one big question and two big issues and decide between three options. The one big question is whether you will officiate for anyone who asks you or set some limits.

Why would a pastor not officiate when a couple comes to him to be joined together in holy matrimony? Evangelical pastors have two big issues, not including the latest big issue of whether a church should bless same-sex unions. That is not an issue for evangelicals. For a pastor who takes the Bible as his authority, the two big issues are whether the pastor will perform the ceremony for a couple when one of them, bride or groom, has previously been married and divorced and whether the pastor will join a couple when one or both is not a believer. Every pastor should prayerfully seek the mind of Christ as revealed in His Word. Following are three options a pastor has in dealing with these issues.

The pastor may accommodate anyone who requests the services of the pastor for a wedding. Those who advocate this position see themselves as nonjudgmental ministers to everyone. If they turn anyone away, they fear they will forfeit any opportunity to reach them for Christ. Nor can they teach them the Christian ideal for the home. So whether the couple are Christian or pagan, divorced or never married, some pastors make no distinctions. Besides, some pastors say, they feel obligated as an official of the state in this capacity to shun discrimination. Some argue that when so many couples are living together unmarried, we should be glad to perform *any* marriage ceremony.

Other pastors elect to try to make a judgment based on the circumstances of each case. Jesus mentions an "exception" in Matthew 5:32 and 19:9: "But I tell you that anyone who divorces his wife, *except for marital unfaithfulness,* causes her to become an adulteress, and anyone who marries the divorced woman commits adultery" (5:32, emphasis added). The same exception appears in chapter 19. Jesus taught that divorce was a concession of the Father to grant some protection to victimized wives. But it was never God's desire that men use it as an easy way out of marriage. Some pastors argue that if divorce is allowed in exceptional cases, then remarriage should be allowed also. In deciding on a case-by-case basis, they try to discern who is the "innocent party" in the divorce. Pastors who take this more liberal alternative also tend to be flexible on the question of joining believers with unbelievers. The Scripture says, "Do not be yoked together with unbelievers" (2 Cor. 6:14a). Some pastors will be more flexible on one issue than on the other.

Another option is to interpret these Scriptures in the light of 1 Corinthians 7:10–11: "To the married I give this command (not I, but the Lord): A wife must not separate from her husband. But if she does, she must remain unmarried or else be reconciled to her husband.

And a husband must not divorce his wife." If scriptural grounds for divorce exist, this passage does not seem to leave room for remarriage. This third option, then, is to decline to participate in any marriage that violates this Scripture. That usually means that the pastor will not unite a couple when either the bride or the groom has a former spouse still living. The minister who binds himself to biblical guidelines on the divorce will likely do the same on the matter of joining a believer with an unbeliever. The same passage is clear on both issues: "A woman is bound to her husband as long as he lives. But if her husband dies, she is free to marry anyone she wishes, but he must belong to the Lord" (v. 39).

If you are a beginning pastor, you will do well to study these Scriptures prayerfully and work out a firm statement before facing a couple. It is difficult to decide objectively while facing a starry-eyed man and woman who have already decided to marry. You are not going to change their minds; they will find someone else to officiate. They might or might not appreciate your convictions.

PREMARITAL COUNSELING

I require at least two counseling sessions with a couple who ask me to join them in marriage. In the first session, I talk about things that I know are questions in their minds. They want to talk about calendar, ceremony, and church facilities. I give them copies of wedding application forms with church policies attached. If they have not been to a wedding in our church, we walk to the sanctuary and point out workable arrangements, including a dressing room for the bride. Also, in this first meeting, if I do not know them well, I need to assure myself that they are both born again and wanting to establish a Christian home. I also want to assure myself that it is a first marriage for each of them unless one or both are widowed. My convictions do not allow me to bless any other kind of marriage.

I have a printed list of topics for discussion that I ask them to talk over before the second session. These are not questions that they have to answer for me but things that they should discuss with each other.

1. The most important thing in marriage for me is . . .
2. If I could be different, I would wish for . . .
3. What I want most in my mate is . . .
4. My childhood was . . .
5. My mother is . . . / My father is . . .
6. My relationship with my brother/sister is . . .
7. My definition of an ideal marriage is . . .
8. My goal in life is . . .
9. Love means . . .
10. My religious life can be described as . . .

Couples typically marry at a stage in life when religion is not their top priority. They want a traditional church wedding, but it is often more a cultural than a religious desire. The pastor must help them see that when children come into the family, they are likely to want those children to have religious nurture. If their own Christian heritage was in widely different contexts, what seems unimportant now may be very important later. This problem is compounded when parents and in-laws begin to pressure the couple.

I recommend that each of them complete the ten statements on paper privately before they discuss them. And I suggest that they would find it an interesting exercise to try to anticipate how their intended will complete each paragraph. It might reveal just how well they know each other.

An encouraging concept that is gaining support at this writing is called "covenant marriage." Following is the covenant that this concept advocates:

> Believing that marriage is a covenant intended by God to be a lifelong relationship between a man and a woman, we vow to God, each other, our families, and our community to remain steadfast in unconditional love, reconciliation, and sexual purity, while purposefully growing in our covenant marriage relationship.

The concept provides for serious commitments on the part of the participating couples. And it requires much of their churches and ministers. The couples agree to study a number of Scriptures related to marriage. They take a marriage preparatory inventory designed to identify potential strengths and weaknesses. They commit to at least six sessions of marriage preparation counseling with the minister or someone trained by him. They also agree to join a couples' class in the church.

The congregation is asked to affirm an appropriate marriage policy and to pair the newlyweds with an appropriate mentoring couple. The pastor agrees to preach a sermon series once a year, at least four messages, on the biblical view of marriage and family. If the pastor and the congregation agree to all of the required promises, the church will have a major emphasis in this area.[1]

REHEARSALS THAT RUN SMOOTHLY

One minister friend of mine does not go to wedding rehearsals. He tells the couple, "I know my part; I don't need to rehearse." He has a lady in his church who delights to plan weddings as a ministry. I rarely managed to avoid booking two evenings for each wedding, but I did learn a few things about how to expedite the rehearsal. Following are some things that will help.

In the earlier counseling with the bride and groom, one session is devoted to the wedding ceremony. I know before rehearsal night that it will be a double-ring ceremony, with unity candle, or whatever. We go to the sanctuary and talk about the bride's vision of the ceremony.

On the day of the rehearsal, I meet the wedding party at the appointed hour. I call them to the front of the chapel and begin the rehearsal with prayer. Then I ask each person to introduce himself or herself and tell what part they have in the wedding party. Often, someone will be missing. They are coming from out of town or they are not yet off from work. You can't keep the whole party waiting, so I ask the bride to pick someone to stand in for the missing party. The bride often wants someone to stand in for her also so she can see the vision from different angles.

Then I make a short speech to everyone present; it saves a lot of frustration. With as much good humor as I can manage, I tell them that this evening and the next will be the bride's big event. We all—even the groom—are going to do what she tells us to do. After the wedding, he might be the boss, but tonight we are all present to ensure that *her* dream comes true. Then I stress that she might have some ideas for her wedding that we have never seen before. It will probably be traditional but not necessarily the tradition that we had at our weddings. I then make a clear rule: We all—including the pastor—are going to keep our ideas to ourselves, unless the bride asks for advice. Then I begin to direct the wedding rehearsal according to plan.

The plan is to begin with everyone on the spot where they will be standing for the reading of the vows. I go through the heart of the wedding and straight through to the recessional. When everyone knows where he or she will be standing, the processional becomes more easily understood. There is the lighting of the candles, the seating of the mothers, and the entrance of the minister, the groom, and the best man. Then comes the parade of the bridesmaids and the father of the bride escorting the star of our show. From there, we go through the vows briefly, a second time, if necessary. I give the bride a chance to make changes.

When she is satisfied, everyone is off to the rehearsal dinner on time. I don't usually go to that event unless it is a couple with whom I have been particularly close. Rehearsals that run smoothly make for weddings with dignity and beauty.

MINISTER OF GOD AND OF GOVERNMENT

The libertarian tendency of public policy in our times has streamlined marriage laws. Still, the state has a legitimate interest in marriage and family. A marriage license is proper. Society has a valid need to see that some lecher does not take a twelve-year-old girl as his wife. Anyone getting married has a right to know if his or her intended has HIV or some other serious communicable disease. For this reason, most states require a license, a blood test, and a waiting period in which to notify the couple of any problems that surface in the test. The state will set such other restrictions as lawmakers believe to be in the public interest. For example, the law might prescribe that witnesses must be a certain age to sign the certificate.

Ensure that you are properly enrolled as one authorized to officiate at weddings. Get the marriage license in hand and properly filled out before the ceremony. You are responsible for getting the signatures of the bride, the groom, and the witnesses in the proper places. The certificate will include a section for the couple to keep and a part for you to mail to the courthouse. Do it the same day, and you will never worry about missing the deadline.

CHURCH WEDDING POLICIES

A church should have clearly written policies about weddings. The pastor should communicate these policies from the beginning to those who wish to be wed in the church. It would be wise to have a list of appropriate requirements and restrictions attached to the wedding application. The couple should sign a copy that includes what the church offers and what it does not allow. Following are a few things that should be a matter of church policy.

1. The couple applies for calendar use of the church for the rehearsal and the wedding. Will a reception be held at the church? If so, that will also require booking to avoid conflict.

2. Whom to join in holy matrimony should be the pastor's decision. There may be good reasons why you cannot perform the ceremony. We have already mentioned two issues that arise. For some reason, the couple might prefer a former pastor or some other minister to officiate. It is appropriate to accommodate the wedding party and other ministers who might be involved. Courtesy would be served best if the host pastor takes the initiative to invite the visiting minister to his church.

3. Cost of the facilities should be spelled out. Many churches charge members nothing for the use of the facilities even though it is a considerable expense. June weddings in the South are a great drain on the utilities for air conditioning. Nonmembers should pay a reasonable amount to defray expenses. The couple should understand that the facility is not reserved until the fee is paid.

4. *Include the services of a custodian in the fee.* If custodial services are not included, a separate fee should be charged for the extra time and labor involved in moving pulpit furniture and clearing out wedding decor before Sunday services. The custodian's duties should be clearly delineated. Will he wash the punch bowl and a hundred cups? Or will the wedding party provide for kitchen cleanup?

5. *It is best to use church instrumentalists or those approved by the pastor.* Your organist would probably rather give up Friday and Saturday evenings than find out on Sunday morning that all of the stops have to be reset. The pastor knows what to expect if his own pianist or organist is at the keyboard.

6. *The wedding party should be responsible for any damage to the church.* Ruining a thousand dollars worth of church carpet with dripping candles is inexcusable. Nondrip candles cost little more and should be required.

7. *Alcohol should be prohibited.* Most evangelicals will find it offensive for guests to smoke in the church or to drink alcoholic beverages. The couple applying should make it their duty to see that it does not happen. They do need to know this in advance, however, and not discover it while they are popping the cork of a champagne bottle in the church fellowship hall.

8. *Will your church allow the tossing of rice?* Besides being a pagan custom and a great hazard on hard floors, the animal rights people tell us that rice kills our little feathered friends. The birds eat the rice, then drink water. It is a fatal combination. In recent years, we have seen a trend toward tossing bird seed instead of rice.

9. *What about photographers?* Photographers can ruin a wedding in a hurry—especially the self-appointed amateurs with their video cameras. A professional will accept a no-flash rule after the processional during the exchanging of the vows. He can get a great time lapse with candlelight. And after the wedding, he can stage whatever shots he and the wedded couple want.

With a word processor, it is easy to pull up your wedding document, insert the names, and make such changes to the ceremony as the particular wedding might require. It will fit on a single sheet of eight and one-half by eleven-inch paper, folded into four pages to fit into your Bible. My custom has been to sign and date those printouts. Then I put a note on my calendar to mail it to the couple in time for their first wedding anniversary.

If the pastor and the church take care in the ministry of marriage, it can be a joy-filled opportunity to serve. We turn now to another ministry opportunity that, although not often joyful, is still a much-needed service. If a pastor sharpens his skills in the ministry to the bereaved, he will hardly find any duty more blessed.

THE FUNERAL: A MINISTRY TO THE FAMILY

The main purpose of a funeral service is to bring such comfort as we can to hurting hearts. The family and close friends will need help coping with the reality of their loss. A funeral is also an occasion for the community to pay proper respect to the deceased. But the primary purpose is to minister to the family.

1. Visit as soon as possible after the news of a death. It need not be a long visit. There is such a thing as the ministry of presence. Just being there as Christ's undershepherd might be more important than anything you say. Express your sympathy in prayer and Scripture reading. I have found it helpful to those in sorrow if the pastor takes as many decisions off of them as they will allow. I tell them that I will be planning the funeral service to honor Christ and help those who mourn. I tell them that I will be open to suggestions about any favorite Scripture reading they would like to include; otherwise, I will make selections as I think best.

This does two things for the family. It releases them from the burden of a whole range of decisions when they have more to cope with than they can well manage, and it also lets them know that you are open to a request. Often, someone will request a well-marked passage from the Bible of the deceased or ask you to read a poem or a clipping found as a bookmark in the Bible.

2. *Plan the funeral for the glory of God and as a ministry to those who sorrow.* Once I was called to conduct the service of a businessman. He was not at all active in the church but the widow was. Their two young-adult children came to me just minutes before the organ prelude ended. They wanted assurance that the sermon would be short. I assured them that I was always sensitive to that need but read something more in their request. How short? They thought that five minutes would be plenty long enough. I asked, "Is this your mother's request?" It was not, but they thought they knew what their deceased father would prefer. I told them that I would take their request into consideration but pointed out that we needed to consider the widow first, then other family members, and also the whole gathered community who have also suffered a loss.

3. *Meet the family again, just before the funeral service if possible.* If it is in a funeral home, there will be a family room. If the funeral is to be at church, it might be good for the minister to plan to drive to the home where the family is gathering.

4. *Be careful in eulogizing the dead.* Eulogy is coming back into vogue. In the late twentieth century it had all but disappeared. If you risk a eulogy, be honest and kind. Unless the departed was known as a strong Christian, some people will think that you are trying to "preach someone into heaven." If you say anything negative, you add to the family's sorrow when they are looking for solace. If the deceased was not a Christian or was only a nominal church member, the less you say about the deceased, the better.

M. E. Dodd was a pastor in my hometown who was glad to eulogize and was trained in oratory. He was out of town when he learned of a death in the church and returned just in time for the service. He did not even have time to see the casket or greet the family before going to the pulpit. He delivered a fine eulogy, but there was one problem. The deceased was not the prominent lady in his church whom he had in mind but another woman of the same name with a less-than-sterling character. The living woman was glad to know what nice things her pastor would say about her. I don't know how the bereaved family reacted.

THE FUNERAL SERMON

1. Keep it brief. The most frequent request that a grieving family will make is "We don't want a long service." That means any funeral sermon will have to be brief. How long is long enough? Considering that there will be an obituary, Scripture reading, and perhaps a bit of eulogy, ten or twelve minutes is long enough. If the pastor keeps his ministry to twenty or at most twenty-five minutes, the funeral will still last an hour.

2. Keep it biblical. I was a nineteen-year-old pastor when I had my first funeral, and I was scared witless. I shut myself up and prayed desperately for a message to help those who were hurting. The answer to that prayer was an outline that I have used many times since then and shared with pastor friends. It uses 1 Thessalonians 4:13–18 as a text, and the last verse in the King James Version provides the line of direction: "Wherefore comfort one another with these words." The three words of comfort are *return, resurrection,* and *reunion.* Follow the unfolding text, and you will offer comfort based on the Christian assurance of the return of our Lord and the return of our loved ones. The resurrection of our Lord is the basis for our confidence in the resurrection of the dead in Christ. And the reunion that we anticipate also will be with our Lord and with our loved ones: "We . . . shall be caught up together *with them* in the clouds, . . . and so shall we ever be *with the Lord"* (KJV, emphasis added).

3. Keep it simple. Because no time exists to develop a full sermon, a one-point sermon may serve very well. A one-point sermon? Yes. Select a brief text, explain it briefly, illustrate it briefly, and apply it briefly. For example, 1 Peter 5:7 says, "He cares for you." These are the words, by the way, of one of the disciples who woke Jesus from slumber in a terrific storm on the Sea of Galilee, demanding, "Teacher, don't you care if we drown?" (Mark 4:38b). Yes, He cares. Any one of several hymns and poems based on this text will help to make that one point.

THE GRAVESIDE SERVICE

Most funerals end with a committal service at the grave. In some cases, the whole service is at graveside. A chapel service is not always appropriate. Perhaps an aged person outlived all of his or her friends and family. It might be a newborn who lived less than a day. Family and friends might meet the funeral director and minister at the cemetery. This ministry calls for a few special considerations.

1. Start on time but not early. The service will be scheduled for a certain hour. The family will be there early. So will the pastor. Someone will look around and suggest, "I believe everyone is here. Why don't we go ahead?" If you decide to do so, probably another car or two will drive up on time just as you are finishing. You can avoid this awkward and potentially embarrassing moment in a couple of ways. You might remain in your car in sight of the family until closer to the appointed hour. A better solution is to join the family and explain that others might be coming. If the cemetery is a long way from home, as sometimes is the case, travel time requires a greater margin of safety to avoid being late. That means a longer wait at the cemetery for the appointed hour. Dispel the awkwardness of the wait by informal ministry. Once at such a service, we passed the time relating memories of the life we were celebrating. At another service, we sang favorite old hymns. At others, we passed the time in informal visiting.

2. Be brief at the graveside. As in the case of the service in church or funeral chapel, grieving hearts do not need a long-winded preacher. If this service follows a funeral and processional to the cemetery, keep it a simple committal of the remains to the ground. When the family is in place, perhaps seated under a canopy, encourage the others assembled to gather around. Read a brief passage of Scripture and close in prayer. That's enough. My favorite reading at this service is Revelation 21:1–7 on the new heaven and the new earth, where there is "no more death or mourning or crying or pain" (v. 4). Mark your reading so that you do not run over into the lake of fire in verse 8. This is not the time for a text on hell.

What if there has not been a chapel service and the whole funeral is at graveside? Then it might last a few minutes longer. Members of the church and community will probably join the family. You might or might not decide to use the obituary. If you do, try to prepare in advance ways to personalize it so that it does not sound like a fill-in-the-blanks recital of dates and survivors.

WORKING WITH THE PROFESSIONALS

1. The funeral director can be a pastor's friend. If you contact him early, he will help you by fitting the funeral around your schedule. After the arrangements have been made, it would be well to go by and pick up the obituary or clergy card. It will be useful in sorting out names and family relationships. It is also wise to review it in case it includes names that you might need help pronouncing. Get the help of a family member to review it with you. Don't ask the widow or widower or the nearest kin to do this; he or she might be too grieved to be helpful. It is amazing how many typographical errors and other mistakes get on those cards.

2. The funeral chapel is not to be discouraged. In the mid-nineteenth century many funerals were held in the church. If it is a funeral of an active church member, and if the service will be a real worship service, that might still be the best place. Some of the bereaved, however, might have a problem if the funeral is at the church. They tend to struggle with the association of the place and their very negative emotional experience there. I have heard them say, "I can't come back to church. All I can see is that casket in front of the pulpit." Today's funeral home has a convenient chapel.

3. Learn the local customs. The funeral director can help a new pastor avoid embarrassing missteps. And when you move to a new community, he can help you learn local traditions. Customs do vary from one community to another. In south Louisiana, for example, I learned that the wake is still common. It sometimes lasts all night, with or without festivities. In cities such as New Orleans, the crime problem is changing that tradition. Some funeral homes close their doors in the early evening. Ironically, it was a crime problem that made the wake customary: In the nineteenth century, body snatchers stole bodies to meet the demand of medical students.

Cultural and racial variables also exist, at least in the South, where most of my experience has been. Black church tradition might delay the funeral a week or more. And the need for brevity might not be so important.

4. *Music is a solace for the sorrowing.* The minister should encourage music with a spiritual, eternal message. Sometimes a surviving spouse will request a sentimental love song from their courtship days. The pastor might not appreciate it, but he is there to help those who are grieving. There is a growing acceptance of taped music in funeral home services. The director will have all of the old hymns and a selection of other music—patriotic, sentimental, and requiem. When there is a live soloist, I invite him or her to come to the pulpit with me. Some people prefer to sing from behind a screen.

We turn a page now to a new theme: ministerial ethics. We will discuss the discipline of what is good or bad, right or wrong for a minister. Some moral duties and obligations pertain to the parson in particular.

chapter nine

MINISTERIAL ETHICS

PETER DRUCKER, THE BUSINESS GURU and pioneer of management theory, has often insisted, "There is no such thing as 'Business Ethics,' there is only ethics."[1] What about ministerial ethics? Certainly, ethical standards that apply to all people apply to ministers. But the church has a right to expect that ministers be held to the highest standard. So does the world. In addition, certain ethical issues are unique to the ministerial office. This chapter addresses ethical issues in two areas: issues of a minister dealing with a church and issues dealing with other ministers in the wider community.

DEALING WITH A CHURCH

We have already discussed in chapter 2 the protocol of a pastor considering a church and being considered by one. Some of those matters are ethical issues; others are common courtesies. Deal with one church at a time. Deal only with a church that is dealing with one candidate at a time. Decide if you will accept a call before a vote is taken. In most cases, the vote should be taken on the day of candidating. The following are ethical issues that a minister will face in finding and fulfilling his calling in a church. Those in an episcopal tradition such as the Methodist church will find that some of this is of academic interest only.

1. *There is a right way to seek a place of service.* Should a candidate recommend himself? It once was taboo, but, as we mentioned in an earlier context, some churches now advertise for résumés. If you decide to send your own résumé, do so openly and honestly. Don't send it anonymously, and don't send it with a dishonest cover letter. When I was a college student, a collegiate minister invited me to write any church in which I might be interested and recommend myself, signing his name. I appreciated the confidence and told him so, but I did not accept his offer.

Your résumé should include the names, addresses, and phone numbers of established pastors and other leaders who know you and will give you a good recommendation. You need the permission of each person on your reference list. Three or four names are usually enough. Understand that most churches still consider only recommendations and not direct applications. If you ask a minister friend to recommend you to a particular congregation, you put him in an awkward position. He might not think that your ministry gifts fit that church's needs. Should he tell you so or send a letter that is less than candid?

2. *Openness is the watchword in accepting a call.* By the time a congregation votes to extend you a call, you have interviewed before the pulpit committee two or three times and preached in the church. You probably visited with different groups during the day and answered a lot of questions. Hopefully, you found answers to your own questions. The vote should be the same day, but some churches delay it a week or more to give official notice to the members. By the time you leave the field, you should know if you will accept a call to that field of service. It is dishonest to tell them that you are praying about it if indeed you are keeping them on the string while you wait to see if a more attractive church will make an offer.

Before the committee asks the church to vote to call you, they should know if you are inclined to accept a call. Unless the vote is seriously divided or otherwise a problem, you should give an affirmative answer without delay. Two or three days is plenty of time if you have not waited until now to begin to pray.

If the vote on your call is less than unanimous, you might take a little more time to assess the opposition. Was it a secret ballot or a standing vote? Perhaps children were voting with less than mature judgment. Perhaps a group wanted an older pastor. You will need honest counsel from leaders in the church to help you assess the nature of the negative vote. The church might have been seriously divided into cliques before your visit. Will they unite under your leadership? If the division is strong, perhaps God is saying that you are not the one to draw them together.

Sometimes a church with a congregational government will have a near unanimous vote on a secret ballot. Then someone who voted in the negative will move that the congregation make it a unanimous vote. Hopefully, the moderator will explain that this is not asking anyone to change his or her vote. The candidate will be informed of the numbers in both ballots. But the second vote is a vote to say that we all accept the will of the majority, and we will all support the new pastor if he agrees to come.

3. *Blessed is the young minister who has opportunity to serve an internship.* If you are so blessed as to be an assistant pastor, loyalty to your pastor is foundational. He is a human; he will be imperfect. Accept him warts and all. If he is of such flawed character that you cannot give your undivided loyalty, you should quietly resign. In that case, if you tell your pastor why you are leaving, be sure to tell no one else. This rule applies if you begin as a youth pastor, an assistant to the pastor, or any other understudy. It can be a great learning opportunity to serve with a seasoned pastor. You will learn things that are not taught in college or seminary. Books are good and necessary, but experience is still the best teacher.

4. *Use caution with any physical show of affection toward church members.* It is regrettable that we are living in a time of suspicion toward ministers. One generation ago, a pastor had to be very careful about showing affection to the ladies. He couldn't hold on too long when he was shaking a girl's hand. Now he is regarded with suspicion if he hugs other men or children of either sex. Perhaps in some communities this is not the case, and I'm sure that some personalities can get by with hugging and kissing everyone. The caution, nevertheless, needs a hearing. When in doubt, don't.

5. *The pastor's relationship to the official board might be a special challenge.* Every church has them. They might be called deacons or elders or directors or something else. But the church looks on them as an official board. The pastor is ordinarily a member of every board or committee by virtue of his office. That is the meaning of *ex officio*. Some traditions, however, think of the pastor as a teaching elder and of this body as the ruling elders. That was John Calvin's distinction. In any communion, the need for oneness of heart is crucial, and the potential for disharmony is present in every church. A wise pastor will seek to cultivate a spirit of teamwork.

Ira Peak, a pastor who was a mentor to me as his associate, told me of a church he served in Oklahoma. Soon after his arrival, the newly elected chairman of deacons came to see him. He said, "Pastor, in this church it has long been the tradition that the chairman of deacons serves as leader of the opposition. If it's all right with you, I'd rather not take that role." It was certainly all right with "Parson Peak." They both enjoyed a wonderful tenure of peace and progress.

We are in danger of letting our culture shape our concept of church government. In America, we have a system of checks and balances in civil government, and party spirit is celebrated. In the New Testament, however, it is not. Paul appealed to the church at Corinth in the name of the Lord Jesus Christ to end their partisan factions. He called them to "agree with one another so that there may be no divisions among you and that you may be perfectly united in mind and thought" (1 Cor. 1:10). It is an ideal that is not often realized. What can a pastor do to promote teamwork and cooperation between himself and his official board?

The pastor can regard them as fellow laborers in God's vineyard. For example, suppose that a decision has to be made about a church program. The wise pastor will discuss the options with other leaders in the church. Let them suggest solutions. The pastor will probably have his own plan tentatively framed. He might find suggestions from the others that will fit nicely into his proposal. Usually, the pastor's plan will be accepted as their plan. If a different plan wins support, the pastor should not take it as a personal attack.

A pastor should get to know the lay leaders personally. Visit in the home of each one as soon as possible. How old is he or she? How long has she been a Christian? How long has he been in this church and on this board? How does he regard his duties as a church leader? What is her idea of the role of the pastor? What are their vocations? Or, because many of these mature leaders will be retired, what was his career? Get to know their families also. You will find that some men who delight to flex their authority muscles at church are hen pecked at home. Others are frustrated with a dead-end job at work. You might not be able to change those situations, but it helps you to understand them.

It is appropriate to recognize the work of lay leaders publicly. Problems, however, are best handled privately. Praise, if genuine and deserved, should be as public as possible, and that is the only kind of praise a pastor should give. Flattery is a form of lying. Although some people might enjoy receiving it, almost all will recognize it for what it is.

If lay leaders don't know how to do their job, it is the pastor's duty to teach them. Two key passages for training deacons are in the New Testament. Acts 6:1–4 is surely the story of the first deacons. It is true that in this text they are not called "deacons," but their work is described by the Greek verb that provides our English word *deacon*. "It would not be right for us to neglect . . . the word of God in order *to wait* on tables" (v. 2, emphasis added). And the noun form of that same word is used in describing the priority of the apostles: to give their "attention to prayer and *the ministry* of the word" (v. 4, emphasis added). There was a division of labor. Both apostles and deacons were ministers. The church accepted the new office and enjoyed the blessing of God that followed.

The other key passage is 1 Timothy 3:8–13. Paul instructed Timothy in the qualifications for deacons and their wives. Most of the guidelines are character qualities. And reputation is very important. Surely a church should look to these Scriptures in selecting leaders and not to worldly standards such as success in business and financial prosperity.

OUR DEALINGS WITH OTHER MINISTERS

1. *There is a right and a wrong way to deal with former pastors.* Don't criticize or entertain criticism of your predecessor. You might be walking in the path he walked, but you are not walking in his moccasins. Every pastor has gifts for ministry, but not all of them have the same gifts or in the same measure. Your predecessor had both strengths and weaknesses, and so do you.

Invite your predecessor to revisit the church. He has friends there who will be glad to see him and hear of his ongoing ministry. If you are still new, some members will want their former pastor to come to conduct a wedding or a funeral. You should make him feel welcome. In fact, as we suggested when talking about weddings, you should be the one to issue the invitation. Paul did not see Apollos or Peter as his competitors. The carnal church at Corinth rallied to their favorite, but Paul urged them to see the whole team. One planted the seed, another watered it, but God made it grow (see 1 Cor. 3:1–6; cf. 1:1–17).

When you become a "former pastor," there is a right way and a wrong way to deal with your former church and her new shepherd. If you visit your old church field, visit the pastor first. If someone in that church invites you to return for a wedding or a funeral, ask the blessing of the new pastor before you agree to come. Better yet, the family seeking your service should request that their current pastor invite you.

A departing pastor should tell his replacement nothing unless he asks. Then share charitably little about individuals in the church. Someone who gave you a hard time might repent and determine to make it up to the next pastor. After I had been some months in a pastorate, a woman in the church came to talk to me. She expressed deep sorrow for the way she treated her former pastor, my predecessor. She was convicted particularly about the part she had played in pressuring him to move. She determined never to take part in such a movement again.

The question sometimes arises about the wisdom of a retiring pastor or an interim pastor remaining in the church after his successor arrives.

I will give no firm rule here because I have seen it work well and not so well. It is difficult for a shepherd to let another person come to take care of the flock that he has long considered his own. And it is not always easy for the new pastor to accept that overshadowing presence. The grace of God that Paul urged on the Corinthians will be needed. Everyone will need to have the mind of Christ and realize that Paul and Apollos are both servants of Christ (1 Cor. 1–2). It is His flock; we are His undershepherds.

2. Be considerate of visiting ministers. When you invite a minister to come to your pulpit, be a gracious host. If he is flying in, meet him at the airport or see that someone does. Take him to his room. Give him time to rest and study. Don't stuff his schedule full of your own pastoral duties, and don't make promises that he must keep.

David M. Dawson Jr. wrote a prize-winning book for new pastors nearly fifty years ago. It is now out of print but was very helpful to me as I prepared for ministry. In it, he told of being invited to preach a series of revival services. He arrived on the field to discover that his host had committed him to all sorts of promises. He was to award a prize to the person who brought the most new people to the meeting. He was giving a Bible to every child who attended all of the sessions of the conference. On "family night," he would give a picture to the class with the largest attendance. On "men's night," there would be a book for the man who brought the most men. The week cost him considerably more than the love offering.[2]

When you invite a minister to visit, don't send him away empty. If he agreed to come for a freewill offering, at least have a check for his expenses ready before he departs. When you are the visiting minister, mind your manners as well. Accept graciously whatever hospitality is extended. This applies to the honorarium also. The church might not be able to entertain you as royalty. Gluttony is one of the seven deadly sins in early church tradition, and so is avarice. Don't be guilty of either.

3. Should the evangelical pastor be a part of interfaith organizations? Perhaps this issue is one of those questionable matters to which the New Testament rule applies: "Each one should be fully convinced in his own mind" (Rom. 14:5c). But I will give my opinion. Most of these organizations will cast a wide net and draw in religious leaders of all kinds, including those who deny Christ. Can you join with unbelievers without compromise? I visited our local ministerial alliance a couple of times but could not in good conscience bring myself to join.

Jerry Falwell tried to solve the problem with a separate organization for issues that related to society in general. In the 1970s and 1980s, the Moral Majority was an alliance open to cooperation with Jews and other non-Christians. They united in their common hope to reverse America's moral decline. At the same time, the Thomas Road Baptist Church, Liberty University, and related organizations would not allow any deviation at all from rather strict Fundamentalism.

4. *The church is greater than one denomination.* Jesus prayed for unity among believers. That prayer in John 17 must become our prayer too, if it is ever to be answered.

> My prayer is not for them alone. I pray also for those who will believe in me through their message, that all of them may be one, Father, just as you are in me and I am in you. May they also be in us so that the world may believe that you have sent me. I have given them the glory that you gave me, that they may be one as we are one: I in them and you in me. May they be brought to complete unity to let the world know that you sent me and have loved them even as you have loved me. (vv. 20–23)

Jesus did not pray for uniformity but for unity. He did not ask for church union but for unity. There is a classic and vivid distinction between the two: You can tie a cat and a dog together by their tails and have union but not unity. In America, we magnify minor distinctive doctrines and make them major dividing lines. Most of the things that keep evangelicals divided are minor matters. What is the proper form of church government? What is the proper mode of baptism? In many foreign cultures, however, Christians are a distinct minority. In such lands, a strong bond binds together all who honor the name of Christ Jesus.

I was pastor in southern Louisiana for a few years in the late 1970s. At that time, the charismatic renewal was making a significant impact on the Roman Catholic population, a sizable majority of the local populace. Many Roman Catholics were coming to know Christ in a personal new-birth experience. At the time, newly elevated Pope John Paul II welcomed their religious vitality. In an earlier time, when Roman Catholics were born again, they left the church and sought membership in evangelical churches. Not this time. They were hungry for Bible study, however, and not sure how to go about it. Someone suggested to a couple of the local lay leaders that I might be able to help them. It was my privilege to teach them how to use simple Bible study tools like a concordance and a commentary. None of them joined my church, but they continued to lead other Catholics to a saving knowledge of Christ and to nurture them in Bible knowledge.

Pastors bear the burden of responsibility for division or unity in the body of Christ. Most of the laity care little for what they consider to be minor differences. The world notes our divisions, however. It is a scandal for which they hold us in contempt and rightly so. James rebukes us for the "envy and selfish ambition" in our hearts. He bids us abandon this worldly wisdom in favor of the wisdom from heaven that is not only pure but "peace-loving, considerate, submissive, full of mercy and good fruit, impartial and sincere" (James 3:13–17). Paul's letters often appeal for unity. For example, Ephesians 4:3: "Make every effort to keep the unity of the Spirit through the bond of peace."

5. Pastors should think more of cooperation and less of competition. Sheep stealing is a crime; some pastors should be under arrest. I recall a brother in a city where we both served as pastors. When he made hospital calls, he did not call on just his flock. He made it his policy to call on everyone he could find of his denomination. He gave them all the same pitch: "You ought to come to our church." Later, although his church was growing and apparently doing well, he came under great pressure to resign or be fired. Then he pleaded with all of his fellow pastors to come to his rescue. They probably would have been more eager if he had been a part of the team, rather than a rival.

A fellowship that has greatly enriched my life in the past two decades is a Thursday morning men's prayer breakfast. It is hosted by an attorney who serves as moderator for a dozen or more men. The mix changes from time to time as men come and go, but about half of us are ministers and the others are an assortment of occupations. About half of the men are of the same denomination as the leader and half are not. The ages range from teens to very senior. In recent years, we are black and white in a community where the Ku Klux Klan still has a strong following. We are a band of brothers who draw strength from each other and bear each other's burdens. That is how it ought to be in the body of Christ.

The next chapter focuses on a special kind of minister—the bivocational pastor. This is a great and essential ministry that many pastors will experience at some time in their career.

chapter ten

THE BIVOCATIONAL PASTOR

MERLE DEAN PRATER HAS BEEN the pastor of Promise City Church of Christ in Centerville, Iowa, since 1968. He is also a farmer, as was his father. The church averages about thirty-five in Sunday morning worship and has never paid him much. He earns his living raising Black Angus cattle and feed grains. He worked for a while in the John Deere factory also. He is in his seventies now and is slowing down. When he was going full tilt, it was not unusual for him to work sixty hours a week on the farm and another twenty in pastoral duties.

Dennis W. Bickers worked in a factory. He had a few months' experience as an interim pastor when a struggling church asked him if he thought that there was any hope for them. He took their challenge. He changed to the night shift to take classes at a Bible school in Louisville, Kentucky. He took a half load of academic studies on top of his church duties and factory job. After four years, he transferred to a university that gave him credit for the courses he had completed. He took early retirement from the factory and began to manage a family business while continuing the pastorate of Hebron Baptist Church. The church has progressed, and the busy pastor has managed, with all of his other responsibilities, to write a very helpful book, titled *The Tentmaking Pastor: The Joy of Bivocational Ministry*.[1]

In the first one hundred years of American history, the overwhelming majority of pastors earned their living by farming or other occupations alongside the people whom they served. Today, it is a mixed picture, depending on which church tradition is counting. Nearly half of all 365,000 Christian ministers in the United States have a second vocation. Fewer than 8 percent of United Church of Christ ministers engage in a second occupation. Fifteen percent of Episcopal clergy are self-supporting. Until World War II, most Southern Baptist pastors were bivocational. Now it is about one-third. More than 80 percent of black Baptist pastors are bivocational. Probably most churches in the United States were started by bivocational ministers.[2]

SHOULD ALL MINISTERS BE BIVOCATIONAL?

Some people insist that all pastors should be self-supporting. They believe that the church should never compensate them at all. They consider a paid minister to be a "hireling" such as Jesus contrasted with the true shepherd (John 10:11–13). In Jewish tradition, the rabbi could not receive pay for teaching the law; he earned his bread in some other occupation.

Nonetheless, the example of Jesus and the Twelve seems quite clear. They traveled about from one town and village to another preaching the gospel of God's kingdom. A number of women who had been cured and otherwise blessed by His ministry followed them. "These women were helping to support them out of their own means" (Luke 8:3b). Men of means also provided hospitality. For example, Jesus invited Himself to supper at the home of the chief tax collector, Zacchaeus (19:5). The encounter with Jesus so changed the life of Zacchaeus that he publicly promised to give half of his wealth to the poor. Is it stretching the imagination to suppose that some of that offering went to support his Savior? Paul's discourse on this theme seems clear: "The Lord has commanded that those who preach the gospel should receive their living from the gospel" (1 Cor. 9:14).

The *Didache,* or *Teaching of the Twelve Apostles,* is a document that was discovered in 1875 and is usually dated as early as the second century. It warns against itinerant false prophets who pretend to give a

Spirit-inspired utterance, saying, "Give me money, or other things." The church was told not to listen to them (*Didache* XI). "But every true prophet that willeth to abide with you is 'worthy of his food.' . . . Therefore thou shalt take and give to the prophets every firstfruit of the produce of the winepress and the threshing floor, of oxen and sheep" (*Didache* XIII).[3]

Then some people will ask, "Should *any* minister be bivocational?" Paul answered that question also in 1 Corinthians 9:14. It is right and proper that those who receive the spiritual ministry should return material blessing to the minister. But the minister is not bound to accept that arrangement. Sometimes, a valid reason exists to decline financial support from those to whom we minister. And some places, of course, those who receive the ministry are unable to support the minister.

Another text that sometimes troubles the two-job pastor is 2 Timothy 2:4: "No one serving as a soldier gets involved in civilian affairs." Is the secular occupation a distraction from sacred duties? If he accepts gifts, is the pastor not trusting God to supply his needs? These are valid questions. Paul himself returned to his trade of tentmaking from time to time. A pastor might be a tentmaker for several reasons, including the following.

1. *A pastor should not be ashamed to take an outside job in time of financial need.* It is also appropriate for the minister to earn his living at an ordinary "secular" job while he is preaching the gospel. This would be especially true when the ministry is missionary in nature. We don't expect pagans to support a Christian ministry.

Every Jewish boy learned a trade as part of his education. Paul's hometown of Tarsus in Cilicia was famous for making and selling tents. It was a natural choice of trade for him. Paul used his manual trade to support himself when the support of the churches was slow in coming. Remember that no electronic banking existed in the first century. The Roman postal system was for official government use only. Paul had to depend on a Christian group traveling many dangerous miles with a cash gift. "When Silas and Timothy came from Macedonia, Paul devoted himself exclusively to preaching" (Acts

18:5). Apparently, Paul did the same thing at Thessalonica. He reminded them that it was his apostolic prerogative to expect support: "We could have been a burden to you, but . . . we worked night and day in order not to be a burden to anyone while we preached the gospel of God to you" (1 Thess. 2:6–9).

2. Outside employment can set an example of industry. At least part of the time in Paul's three-year ministry at Ephesus, his own hands supplied his own and his companions' needs. He tells why: "In everything I did, I showed you that by this kind of hard work we must help the weak, remembering the words the Lord Jesus himself said: 'It is more blessed to give than to receive'" (Acts 20:35). This example is all the more remarkable when we recall that cultured Greeks despised manual labor and looked down on those who engaged in it. Paul, however, enjoyed the more blessed status of being a giver.

3. The name of Christ and the image of the gospel ministry sometimes is better served by being bivocational. Paul belabored this point in writing to the Corinthians. He insisted on his apostleship. He claimed a right to food and drink for himself and for a wife if he chose one. He pointed to the policy of the other apostles, including Peter and James. He argued from the analogy of a soldier who is paid for his service. One who plants a vineyard or one who tends a flock has a right to the fruit of his labor. He appealed to the law: "Do not muzzle an ox while it is treading out the grain" (1 Cor. 9:9; cf. Deut. 25:4). He argued that he and his companions, who sowed spiritual things among the Corinthians, were not out of line if they expected a material harvest. Others have this right of support; shouldn't the apostle have it all the more (1 Cor. 9:11–12)? He cited the Mosaic Law, which provided food from the temple for those who worked in the temple (v. 13) and concluded, "In the same way, the Lord has commanded that those who preach the gospel should receive their living from the gospel" (v. 14).

At Corinth, however, Paul did not use any of these rights. "On the contrary, we put up with anything rather than hinder the gospel of Christ" (v. 12b). It is appropriate for those who receive the benefit of spiritual ministry to provide material support to the minister. And it is appropriate for the minister to receive such support. But it is also appropriate for him to decline it if it is offered. It is not always better for the minister to devote full-time to the ministry.

BLESSINGS OF BIVOCATIONAL MINISTRY

1. The pastor is not wholly dependent on financial support from the church. The foremost reason for having a second job is almost always financial. A new church does not have the budget to provide an adequate salary. An old church has lost its population base in the rural community. With two salaries, the pastor is not totally dependent on either income. He might be able to own his home and build equity over time. If he loses one job, he still has income; if he keeps the secular job, he might have an adequate income. It might be an advantage to the pastor if the church knows that he is not subject to the leverage of those who hold the purse strings.

2. The struggling church is not so burdened that most of the budget goes to one expense. Money is free to flow to other ministries and needs, including mission work, building, insurance, and literature. Some churches find that they can add other staff members, perhaps also bivocational, to serve in youth, music, nursery, or custodial duties. A trained bivocational minister will probably be more effective than an unpaid volunteer.

3. The pastor is better able to lead by example. If he has another forty-hour week and can make time for church ministry, so should other church members. Such a church knows that the ministry is not a one-man job. Members might be more willing to pitch in and share the work of the ministry as the New Testament teaches. One of the hardest tasks of the typical full-time pastor is to overcome the false notion that the ministry is the work of the paid professional.

4. The second job might be as personally satisfying as a hobby. While living in my hometown and still finishing my seminary work, the house I was renting came on the market. I bid against the prospect of moving out, and the sellers favored my offer. Two years later, I moved to another city for my first full-time pastorate. I decided to keep my first house and let the rent pay the mortgage. It was an era of rapid escalation of real estate values. In a few years, the income was twice as much as the amortization and other expenses. It occurred to me that this was a way to build retirement income. Reading about real estate investments became a hobby. It gave my mind a needed break from ministry burdens. It taught me more about business than I could have learned in a second college career. I added other properties, which did supplement church support.

5. *The bivocational pastor can see the reality of the layman's world as the full-time pastor seldom does.* In church work, we never hear a vulgar or blasphemous word. But in their jobs, our people hear such talk every day. A secular job helps us appreciate what our people face in the workplace, and we are better able to help them deal with temptations of sexual immorality, dishonesty, and shady business dealings when we, too, come and go in the same workplace. The layman knows that his bivocational pastor can identify with his struggles. As a bonus, the pastor meets unsaved and unchurched people who need to be reached. Most of us have a circle of influence in friends, family, and workmates. If our place of work is only the church, we have very few personal contacts for evangelism. The two-job pastor, on the other hand, can appreciate the Great Commission's "as you are going" facet as no cloistered professional ever can.

6. *There is a rhythm in moving from one job to another.* If the two jobs are very different from one another, that can be an advantage. When I was in seminary, I also served a weekend pastorate. Academic study and pastoral work were very much alike. Both were people oriented. Both demanded much Bible study and theology, with deadlines to meet. At the same time, I had a job several nights a week at a warehouse. At a regional distribution center, I loaded eighteen-wheel trucks that went to department stores over several states. It was hard manual labor, but it required practically no mental exertion at all. It was just what I needed—physical exercise and mental relaxation. A classmate worked the same shift, and we rode together. Some of the other men wondered how we could end our shift by sprinting two hundred yards to the parking lot. When I got home at midnight, I didn't need to be rocked to sleep. Nor did I need to schedule jogging or other exercise into my routine.

7. *Bivocational ministers are available to consider serving a struggling church.* Perhaps you would enjoy the challenge of pioneering a new church. You might live in the Bible Belt where a church or two is on every corner. In much of Canada, the United Kingdom, and the Western United States, though, the evangelical voice is practically muted. Bivocational ministry is ideal for church planting. Get your training for ministry and a marketable skill at the same time. Then plant your life where you can plant churches.

Not all struggling churches are new, of course. Some churches are in transitional neighborhoods or declining communities. They might have property and a fine building they can no longer fill with people. Opportunity knocks. The bivocational pastor might be just the one to answer the door.

BURDENS OF BIVOCATIONAL MINISTRY

Some of the most common complaints of bivocational pastors are also problems for their full-time brothers. There is never enough time to do all that needs to be done. The pastor's family is likely to be shortchanged in the squeeze. And they experience frustration from a desire to do more than is humanly possible. But some burdens seem to weigh particularly on the person with two jobs.

1. *Some bivocational ministers suffer an identity crisis.* Am I a minister who has a second job, or am I a factory worker who preaches on the side? Some bivocational pastors feel like second-class servants of the King of Kings. They think, sometimes with good reason, that denominational leaders and their full-time brothers treat them with disdain.

2. *Frequent conflicts occur between the two roles.* If the secular employer is unwilling to allow a flexible work schedule, the pastor may not be able to respond to an emergency. He has trouble scheduling funerals. He can't attend the pastors' conference or take time to fellowship with a pastoral peer group. He can't schedule denominational conventions and training events. If he is a witness at work, he might be downgraded in performance reviews for "preaching" to coworkers.

The pastor/employee can condemn himself for the inability to give 100 percent to both jobs. One pastor confessed that a widely known personal weakness of his hurt his testimony. The world holds ministers to a higher standard.

3. *Having two salaries might tempt a pastor to assume an inappropriate spirit of independence.* When problems arise in the church, he doesn't have to stay and work them out. He can walk away without waiting for another church to open to him. He can do the same with his secular job. Many pastors would envy such independence, but it is not always an advantage. The pastor needs the self-discipline to stick out tough times. Running seldom solves a problem.

4. *A bivocational minister has trouble shifting between roles.* If the second job is in a factory, the worker is a cog in the assembly line. No initiative is allowed. But among the church job, the pastor is expected to lead. I know a pastor with a military background who is still in the reserves. His leadership style is strictly assign and command. Fortunately, his church accepts this part of his personality.

5. *When it comes time to change one job, what about the other?* Even if there are nearby options, churches are reluctant to consider the pastor of a neighboring church. Or administrators in the secular job may demand that their employee transfer. Pastors face a similar problem when their children don't want to leave friends at school or church. It is twice the problem for the pastor with two jobs.

6. *Managing time and setting priorities can be a special problem.* Every pastor faces the problem of keeping a balance in life. How can the pastor be all that he should be and do all that he should do with two sets of work responsibilities? One thing that will help is a thoughtful ranking of priorities. Tentmaking pastor Dennis Bickers suggests five focal points, in this order: (1) God, (2) family, (3) church, (4) secular job, (5) self.[4]

Usually, the secular job at forty hours a week pays most of the bills. A small pastorate might expect little more than weekend commitment. Other pastors give forty to fifty hours a week to pastoral ministry and still need to supplement their income. A part-time job might meet that need. If a pastor keeps the will of God at the top of his list and self-gratification at the bottom, the other demands will likely fall into place. Such a minister should be able to do both jobs well without sacrificing his family.

HOW TO BECOME A BIVOCATIONAL CHURCH PLANTER

In chapter 2, we discussed starting churches. This kind of ministry is well fitted for the bivocational pastor. Gary Farley works in a mission organization that specializes in church planting. He encourages young ministers to consider a career of starting churches as did Paul and Silas and Barnabas and others in the New Testament. He recommends a five-step plan to students preparing for such a ministry. I have tailored points to make the list more useful to pastors in a broader range of evangelical traditions.

1. *Get a portable skill.* Prepare to be both pastor and provider. Get credentials to qualify for work to support yourself wherever God wants you to serve. In the New Testament world, every Jewish boy was trained in a manual skill. Paul was apprenticed to a tentmaker, no doubt. Carpenters, electricians, and plumbers are needed nearly everywhere. Bankers, computer technicians, and teachers can usually find work. Get your credentials in a vocation that you can take wherever you go. Dale Holloway was in college studying to be an elementary school teacher when God called him into ministry. He continued his education on two tracks. After graduation, he spent nearly thirty years as a teacher and a preacher. Now he is a consultant in bivocational ministry.

2. *Cultivate a geographical area.* China is not open to Christian missionaries, yet people with skills in teaching and in business are welcome in China. Suppose that you have a burden for the people in the Great Plains, where evangelical churches are relatively few. Gary Farley notes that several bank cards do their billing from Sioux Falls, South Dakota. You might get training in computers and work your way through school in a bank setting. You will have the credentials for the secular job you need. You might go to South Dakota as a summer missionary, where you can meet pastors and missionaries who will

encourage your vision. They will also be ready to help you find a place to plant a church when you are ready. One of them might want you to come as an unpaid (or minimally paid) staff member until they are ready to plant another church. You will have a close sponsor to give your work authenticity.

3. *Get the training you need for ministry.* The mission field is not a place for amateurs. Get your college degree and theological training. Six or eight years of school is not too long to get ready for a ministry of thirty or forty years. You might need to be mentored as you work on a church staff. Learn about cross-cultural communication. Learn how to win souls, how to start a church, and how to train workers. The woodsman does not consider wasted the time spent sharpening his ax. If you have not become a pastor by the time you are thirty, remember that Moses spent forty years learning Egyptian culture and forty years more learning the life of a Midianite nomad. Then he was ready to lead Israel out of slavery.

4. *Plan to stay the course.* Depending on your age, you will probably have a career of twenty to thirty years after seminary. One church planter might start a church and stay to grow it into a great congregation. At some point, the pastor would cease to be bivocational. That church might start many other congregations. Another minister will specialize in church planting. A great need exists for the missionary who can plant a church, get it ready for a full-time minister, and then start another one.

5. *Network with people who can guide and undergird your initial efforts.* A home church sometimes is willing to sponsor a member who becomes a missionary. Denominational mission boards and parachurch organizations provide credentials and financial support. Teams are established to go into a needy area. When I was teaching at Liberty Baptist Seminary in Lynchburg, Virginia, the ministry aim was to train young Timothys to plant churches. Students were encouraged to form teams while in school. Typically, a pastor, a minister of music, and a Christian education specialist comprised a team. By the last year in seminary, teams had joined and were praying for a specific community. After graduation they went out together, sometimes as three married couples with children, to form the nucleus of a church.[5]

The need for bivocational ministry always will exist in church traditions that allow for it. Bivocational work has its own peculiar blessings and burdens. God might have a place for you to serve in this capacity. You might need to bloom where you are planted, or the Lord might transplant you to a more fertile field of labor. If so, He will give great joy to those who seek His will.

chapter eleven

THE PASTOR AS TEACHER

A PASTOR IS A TEACHER. There is no decision about whether to cultivate a spiritual gift of teaching. Teaching is part of the job description. "The overseer must be . . . able to teach" (1 Tim. 3:2). A shepherd cannot say, "Feeding the flock is just not my gift."

Paul categorized four spiritual gifts in Ephesians 4:11. The ascended Lord "gave some to be apostles, some to be prophets, some to be evangelists, *and some to be pastors and teachers*" (emphasis mine). The fourth category is pastor-teacher. Some translations are not very clear about whether the list includes four or five offices. Some of these translations predate Granville Sharp's discovery of a translation rule for New Testament Greek relating to the use of the Greek article and conjunction. Based on that rule, we can say with assurance that "pastors and teachers" refers to one office, not two. If you are a pastor, your gift is that of a pastor-teacher. You are the Lord's gift to His church for the exercise of that dual role.

So it is not a question of *if* but *how*. How shall the pastor budget time for teaching and for preparation to teach? And how shall the pastor improve his stewardship of this spiritual gift?

FINDING TIME IN THE CHURCH PROGRAM FOR TEACHING

1. Begin by accepting teaching as a priority of ministry. Richard Baxter in *The Reformed Pastor* (1657) sets two burdens of faithfulness upon the pastor. First, we pastors must think of those in our care; second, we also must also remember that we stand before our Judge.

> I am afraid the day will come when unfaithful ministers will wish they had never known the pastoral charge committed to them. They will rather that they had followed other jobs than be pastors of Christ's flock! For besides their other sins, they will also have the blood of so many souls to answer for.[1]

2. Some pastors use midweek "prayer meeting" as teaching time. Many pastors expound a Bible book on Wednesday evenings. One pastor regularly goes chapter by chapter, verse by verse over as many weeks as the selected book requires.

This is a good plan if you do not let it crowd prayer out of the prayer meeting. My own practice was to teach briefly on prayer every Wednesday. *Briefly,* I say, because talking about prayer is no substitute for praying. A pastor should guard the time for corporate prayer. One would think that people would tire of the same theme every week or that the teacher would run out of something to say on prayer. Not so in either case. I once read somewhere, "Your theology of prayer is your whole theology in summary." I don't remember who said it, but I found it to be so. Through years of pastoral ministry, I delighted in planning one series on prayer after another.

One of my first such series was an idea borrowed from Joe Temple, a pastor and radio minister in Abilene, Texas. He was also a popular conference speaker. At an encampment that I attended, he blessed the listeners with a morning watch series on *The Prayer Life of Jesus in the Gospel of Luke.* We learned that Luke has more to say about the prayer life of Jesus than the other three Gospels combined.

Other Bible texts also provide ample bases for series of studies. Look, for example, at the prayers of Abraham, Moses, Elijah, David, and other Old Testament saints. Trace the prayer life of Peter, John, Paul, and the other apostles. One or two such biographical studies a year will be enough.

There are many ways to teach about prayer. The early church shows evidence of great prayer times in Acts. There are numerous Bible doxologies and benedictions. The Bible knows of great intercessors. The model prayer of Jesus, commonly called "The Lord's Prayer," is a rich mine. It might justify a dozen weeks of exposition. So would the Lord's great High Priestly Prayer recorded in John 17. Another series might be on the five forms of prayer: adoration, praise, intercession, confession, and petition. Later, each of these five could provide at least one series. You will run out of Wednesdays before you run out of texts on prayer. You can also use some of them for Sunday sermons.

3. Some pastors prepare Bible teachers, who adapt the content to assigned age groups. Some pastors even write the lessons they want their teachers to use. I did this for one financial stewardship series. For a season of evangelistic harvesting, I once wrote lesson plans for older children, youth, and adult classes. Much good Bible curriculum material is available now, however. Keep looking until you find what your church needs. If you choose to teach the teachers, schedule a time when they can gather. Decide if you are going to use the same Bible passage for all age groups. If so, you should tailor the application to different age groups. Bible teaching should be both content centered (on the biblical revelation) and pupil centered (on the practical application). We must do more than teach lessons; we must teach people.

4. Some special seasons for teaching should be set aside on the church calendar. My own denomination has promoted a January Bible study for nearly a century. It started in the early twentieth century as a Bible conference in one of our leading churches. Every winter, the pastor invited one or two outstanding guest expositors to come for a week of both morning and evening sessions. The host church invited pastors of smaller churches across the state to come and enjoy their hospitality. Church members provided a bed-and-breakfast in their homes.

The host church enjoyed the teaching of some of the finest Bible teachers in the world.

Eventually, this annual Bible study week spread to other churches. Now our denominational publisher selects one Bible book each year and publishes resources for its study. The pastor has the opportunity to expound that book to his own congregation. Often, a pastor will teach it to his own church and then make his preparation do double duty by teaching it for a pastor friend. The following year, the friend might be his guest teacher.

The schedule that I found best was a Sunday-through-Friday event. I selected texts for preaching from the book for Sunday sermons. I had an extra hour before the evening service for introducing the book. We had two hours blocked out each evening Monday through Friday. Usually, the youth studied the same Bible book with an appropriate teacher. Children studied appropriate Bible lessons in age-group graded classes. The pastor guided the adult conference. We took about fifty minutes for the first session and then took a break for refreshments and fellowship. After the fifteen- or twenty-minute break, we returned for the second session of about forty-five minutes.

A church might schedule another week annually to study a Bible doctrine. Many churches do both events annually. The doctrinal emphasis might focus on a basic doctrine, such as Christology or the Atonement. The pastor might sense a need for the church to study foundations of the faith, one doctrine each evening for a week. Depending on their theological bent, churches might want to schedule a series on the five tenets of Calvinism or Arminianism. As an alternative, some churches schedule such events on successive Sunday evenings.

Even a gifted teaching pastor should occasionally invite a guest teacher. The guest might have a specialty that will advance the Bible knowledge of the congregation. It takes a lot of preparation, for example, to teach the typology of the tabernacle in the wilderness. Some teachers have elaborate models or other visual aids to enhance such lessons. They want to use them more than once. Other teachers specialize in the book of Revelation or Bible prophecy. To teach it to the same congregation repeatedly would be to ride a hobbyhorse. A pastor who stays with his flock year after year will do well to invite a trusted friend to be a guest teacher sometimes.

5. *Teaching from house to house is scriptural.* Paul reminded the elders at Ephesus of how he taught them "publicly and from house to house" (Acts 20:20b). Richard Baxter, the seventeenth-century Puritan pastor, scheduled teaching sessions in the homes of each family in his church, during which he taught Bible truth tailored to their needs. He recommended that every pastor find out how each family is structured, and how the family worships God. Does the head of the family pray in his house? Does he read the Scriptures and otherwise lead his family in worship? Baxter wanted pastors to work at convincing them to do so. He had practical guidance for teaching the head of the family how to teach his family. If they have never learned to pray out loud, perhaps they can begin by reciting set prayers from memory. He also recommended a few books current in his era that he thought would be helpful.[2]

Some people might wonder how one can go into a home and get anyone to turn off the television and open a Bible? If children are in the home, you might start by providing Bible story videos. Some quality productions are available. A church could make a wise investment placing such videos in the church library.

6. *Some pastors use the auditorium Bible class or "pastor's class" approach.* People who will not attend any other class often will come to a class that the pastor teaches. Some people will slip into a large class where they know they will not be called on to lead in prayer or answer a Bible question. Because the class is conducted in the sanctuary, other people who come early for worship will find themselves in it. If they like what they find, they will return.

You start this as a "paper class," meaning that you generate a list of names only. This list comes from the church roll and the people who are not in a regular Bible class. Add names of routine pastoral contacts. The pastor may enlist people wherever he finds them. He could go door-to-door in the community, finding those who are not enlisted. At the door, he can introduce himself and ask two questions.

"Our church believes that everyone needs Bible study. Are you currently enrolled in a Bible class?" If they are not involved with a Bible class, ask the second question: "I'm starting a new auditorium Bible class just for you. May I enroll you in it?" If they allow it, you fill out an enrollment card on the spot. Then you give them a copy. Tell them, "You are now enrolled. This card tells you where and when we meet." A good way to enroll church members is on the telephone. Mail a copy of the completed enrollment form to the family as a reminder.

I used this approach successfully in two churches. Not everyone will enroll, but many people will. Not everyone who enrolls will come to the Bible class, but many of them will. In fact, Andy Anderson, who promoted this approach in the 1970s, found that four or five out of ten who agree to enroll will also show up for class. That is the same ratio of attendance to enrollment in the traditional Sunday school—about 40 percent. So how many people do you want attending your auditorium Bible class? Forty? Simply enroll one hundred.

I don't believe that I could do it now, but when I was a young pastor, I actually built two classes at one time. I taught both classes every Sunday and preached twice too. The first class was an auditorium Bible class for adults of all ages. After morning worship, a class for college students met for lunch and Bible study.

To enlist the college students, I visited the campus on Saturday nights from 10 P.M. until midnight or later, when students were returning from their dates or other recreation. They would not be up on Sunday morning in time for traditional Sunday school or church, so I invited them to come at noon and have lunch and a Bible study with other college students. My wife fixed the lunch. It would be a good hot meal, such as hamburger steak, rice and gravy, green beans, rolls, iced tea, and cake. She prepared it at home, took it to church, and kept it hot until class time.

We were both glad when summer came and the college class ended. Before summer was over, we were glad to be on our way to Virginia to begin teaching seminary. Ah, youth. If you are young, I dare you to start a Bible class—or two.

FINDING TIME TO PREPARE

Spending time in enlistment does not justify sloppy teaching. You must also study the lesson passage thoroughly. And you must construct a thoughtful lesson plan. You must be creative to do a good job of both tasks. Consider the following tricks of the trade to help you redeem the time.

1. *Let your preparation do double duty when possible.* When I taught two Bible classes on the same day, I taught the same Bible book and tailored application to the audience. Earlier in this chapter, I told of a pastor who does a verse-by-verse exposition of a Bible book on Wednesday evenings. His congregation knows that next year he will preach a series of Sunday morning sermons through that same book. He does a thorough job of scholarly study, and his preparation does double duty.

2. *Consider a team approach for major projects.* One year, our selection for the January Bible study was Malachi. I definitely did not have a fat file of material from prior study and preaching on that book. I picked about two-dozen names from the pastors and evangelists in our area. I selected men I thought would be serious about preparing to teach that book. I wrote each man a letter and suggested that we get together for a study luncheon one day a week for about seven weeks. Eight men arranged their schedules for the series of luncheons. I led a discussion at the first meeting on the background material for the book. Then we divided the leadership responsibilities like a seminar along the lines of the six oracles of Malachi. Six men volunteered to guide the group through one oracle each at one of the remaining luncheons. In addition, several members of the group volunteered to attend training clinics, investigate resources such as audio and videotapes on Malachi, and report back to the group. We not only got much more preparation for our investment of time but also thoroughly enjoyed the fellowship.

3. *Multiply yourself as Jesus did.* Jesus invested Himself in the special training of twelve men whom He could send in His name. He sent seventy others, two by two, with His message. Frank Laubach developed

a literacy project that required those who learned lesson one to teach it to someone else before they could get lesson two. The project was highly successful. This approach works best when the pastor seeks to develop skill, as well as just knowledge, in each student. We will look closer at this in the next chapter when we talk about soul winning.

LEARNING FROM JESUS, THE MASTER TEACHER

They called Jesus "Rabbi" and "Master." Both terms were titles of respect afforded to a teacher. By all measures, Jesus was the best of all teachers. If we would teach as Jesus taught, His life must flow through us. Following are some characteristics that marked His life and ought to be in ours too.

1. Jesus' vision encompassed the world. It is truly remarkable that Jesus did all of His teaching from the context of a narrow and exclusive Judaism, but His vision was worldwide. He spoke of "other sheep" that He would bring into the one fold. He wanted His provincial followers to lift up their eyes and look on the fields, which were overripe for harvest among all people.

2. Jesus knew the human heart. He did not need anyone to teach Him what was in the human being. He knew the heart. We must not pass off that fact as a supernatural insight beyond our capacity. We can and must study human nature prayerfully. If we are concerned with only teaching lessons, we will study our lessons. But if we would reach human hearts, we must study our pupils.

3. Jesus mastered the subject. We must know Christ personally—not just facts about Him—to follow Him in this mastery. More and more we must become experts on one Book, and the Bible is such a book that no one can ever learn it all. A passage we study this week will yield new and fresh insights into the new life context of next week.

4. Jesus had an aptitude for teaching. This is a spiritual gift, but it is a gift that we must exercise and cultivate. Jesus knew how to take aim in teaching. He sometimes appealed to altruism and sometimes to self-interest. He pointed to future reward and punishment. Jesus used parables and proverbs. Note the vivid imagery in His speech. There must have been a chorus of chuckles at His description of a man's straining his drinking water lest he unwittingly swallow a ceremonially unclean gnat. Then the same fanatic swallows an unclean camel in one gulp. We cloud the minds of our hearers with abstract Latin terms such as *transcendence* and *immanence*. Jesus, however, used down-to-earth language: "I tell you, do not worry.... Look at the birds of the air; they do not sow or reap or store away in barns, and yet your heavenly Father feeds them. Are you not much more valuable than they?" (Matt. 6:25–26).

5. *Jesus' life embodied His teaching.* He taught by example when He washed the disciples' feet. He lived what He taught, whether that was love for the Father or love for all humankind, and so must we. Hearing Him pray, one of His disciples said, "Lord, teach us to pray" (Luke 11:1b). He did so, modeling prayer as well as giving a model prayer (vv. 2–4). We, too, must model the Christ life, especially for the young people. "In everything set them an example by doing what is good. In your teaching show integrity, seriousness and soundness of speech that cannot be condemned, so that those who oppose you may be ashamed because they have nothing bad to say about us" (Titus 2:7–8).

HOW TO PREPARE A LESSON PLAN

Preparing to teach a lesson is much like preparing a sermon. Both preacher and teacher must pray and study. The teacher needs a firm grip on the Bible passage. He needs to be able to state the central truth in a clear and uncomplicated sentence just as is necessary in sermon preparation. The preacher or teacher must develop skill in writing a clear aim for each sermon or lesson. It should be stated in terms of what will happen to the hearer. Do not think, "I want to explain the atonement of Christ" but rather, "I want my class members to see Christ in His death as God's way of removing the sin barrier so that they will come to accept God's gracious forgiveness and peace." In either preaching or teaching, it is helpful to make a brief list of life needs that the Bible passage addresses. I like to use the following four-step plan for guiding discussion or other learning activities.

Step 1. Gain the attention of the class and focus it on the lesson at hand. Sometimes a question will do this. It has the advantage of calling for class members' responses. If it is a well-planned question, it will do other things to create learning readiness. I still recall the way my Sunday school teacher began a class when I was an eleven-year-old boy: "What would you think," he asked, "if you saw an older brother eating a candy bar and not sharing with his little brother? He wants the little brother to eat an apple, but the little fellow is begging for the candy bar. What would you think?"

I had an older brother, so I jumped into his trap and volunteered my opinion: "I'd think he was pretty mean and stingy."

Then the teacher continued. "But what if the younger brother is allergic to chocolate? And what if their mother gave the older brother strict orders not to give chocolate to him? What if the older brother would much rather have the apple, but these are the only snacks they have?"

With that, he had our attention and was ready to introduce the lesson on "Judge not, that ye be not judged" (Matt. 7:1 KJV). His lesson starter was centered in life, right where we lived it. It gained our interest immediately and focused it on the very lesson we needed to learn that day. It helped that the attention getter also got the learner involved. Answering a question does that. Step 1 should lead right into the next step, Bible study.

Step 2. Involve the members in Bible study. Lecturing is the easiest way to *prevent* learning. Perhaps the only advantage of the teacher's doing all of the talking is to guarantee that everything goes according to plan. The teacher covers the material planned, keeps on the lesson, and stays on schedule. But it is still the poorest way to teach in most classes. People learn the lesson that they discover for themselves. Give them something to discover. Give them a problem to solve. Guide them to explore those verses in the lesson that relate directly to the lesson aim and the central truth. Give them opportunity to tell what they find in the Scripture. It might not always be the insight you want them to discover, but almost any response is better than no response. Once they begin to participate in the lesson, they have overcome inertia.

The teacher's task is then easier. You can guide them to the appropriate understanding of this passage.

Step 3. Apply the Bible truth to life. The application step might be separate from the discovery step, or the teacher may apply the truth as it is being explained. In either case, plan for both explanation and application. Don't assume that the class can easily apply the idea.

Suppose that you are teaching a passage on honesty and truthfulness. Does this have something to do with a member of the class who earns his living as a salesman? What about income tax time? Should we report all of our income or just that which we think the government might discover? If the application is separate from the explanation, it helps to give a clear, one-two-three list of things to do. These steps apply the Scripture to everyday life. Again, give the learner a chance to suggest how this lesson relates to life.

Step 4. Take a minute to stimulate study of the next lesson. We have too easily given up on expecting people to open their Bibles between Sundays. A part of the teacher's task is to stir them up to *want* to go to the Scriptures.

In the Sermon on the Mount, you taught from Matthew 7:1–6 the lesson on judging today. The next lesson is on prayer: "Ask. Seek. Knock" (vv. 7–12). How will you arouse curiosity about that lesson? You might say: "One time, I was being considered for a job that I wanted very much. I thought that I was ideally suited for the job and that the job was perfect for me. I prayed that God would open that door so I could go in. And I just knew He would. But it didn't happen. The job went to someone else. How do you square something like that with the promise of Jesus, 'Ask and it will be given to you'? That's what we will explore in the next teaching of Jesus in the Sermon on the Mount. Read and think about verses 7–12. Was there a time in your life when you prayed and God came through? Maybe you can tell us about it. And was there something you learned in a time when God surprised you by saying no?"

That introduction of the next lesson takes about a minute. It starts them thinking ahead. It gives them a purpose for study. You could make the suggestion of a more definite assignment for one or more members of the class.

Preaching, teaching, counseling, and caring for the flock: That's a load for a pastor. Providing leadership, equipping the saints, baptizing the believers, marrying couples, and comforting the brokenhearted—is there anything else? Oh yes, there's more. We turn next to the pastor's role in evangelizing and in equipping the church members to evangelize.

chapter twelve

THE PASTOR AS EVANGELIST

SIX MONTHS AFTER YOUNG CHARLES SPURGEON looked to Christ for salvation, he wrote his mother the following letter, which was dated June 11, 1850, just short of his sixteenth birthday.

> Dear Mother:
>
> Truly, indeed, I have much for which to bless the Lord, when I contemplate his Divine Sovereignty, and see that my salvation is entirely of his free electing love. I have more than sufficient to induce me to give myself entirely to him who has bought me and purchased me with an everlasting redemption.
> I have seventy people whom I regularly visit on Saturday. I do not give a tract and go away; but I sit down and endeavor to draw their attention to spiritual realities. I have great reason to believe the Lord is working—the people are so kind and pleased to see me.[1]

Spurgeon grew into the model evangelistic pastor. He was a personal soul winner and an evangelistic preacher without peer. He organized his church and trained for evangelism. He extended his ministry far and wide with the only mass media of his era—newspapers and a few journals. This chapter explores these topics to help a pastor win souls and equip the saints for this work of the ministry. But first, let us put things in historical perspective.

A THUMBNAIL HISTORY OF EVANGELISM

The apostles were not the only evangelists in the New Testament era. Indeed, the first evangelists scattered by persecution from Jerusalem were not apostles. The day the Sanhedrin stoned Stephen, a great persecution broke out against the church. "*All except the apostles* were scattered throughout Judea and Samaria. . . . Those who had been scattered preached the word wherever they went" (Acts 8:1–4, emphasis added). Philip is an example of such a lay evangelist; he preached to multitudes in Samaria and witnessed to one Ethiopian eunuch on the road to Gaza.

Beginning in the second century, the light of true evangelism grew dim, at least as far as recorded history tells us. Such zeal for souls as we find, was often expressed in a sacramental system of infant baptism and the Eucharist. For more than a thousand years—from the sixth century through the sixteenth century—the Roman Catholic Church dominated Western Europe. Much of Eastern Europe came under the domination of Islam, as Muhammad's armies set out to conquer the world. Islamic leaders subjugated both Jews and Christians and pressured them to convert to Islam. Christian forms of worship were restricted and evangelism was forbidden. Syria, Mesopotamia, Persia, Asia Minor, Egypt, and North Africa all fell to the Muslim advance. It looked as if the Christian world would be encircled and destroyed. Then Charles Martel and his Frankish soldiers dealt a crushing reversal to the Muslim advance in the Battle of Tours in 732.

Starting in 1096, the Catholic Church launched crusades to deliver the Holy Land from Muslim control. The pope's emissaries called down vengeance upon the Muslims for oppressing pilgrims in the Holy Land and Christians who lived in Syria.[2]

In the sixteenth-century Reformation under Martin Luther, Philip

Melancthon, John Calvin, Huldreych Zwingli, and John Knox, an emphasis was again laid upon biblical evangelism. In the eighteenth century, God used popular evangelists John and Charles Wesley, and George Whitfield and popular theologian preachers Jonathan Edwards and Gilbert Tennent to bring revival to England and America in the Great Awakening. They set the stage for generations of evangelists and revivalist leaders, from D. L. Moody to Billy Sunday. Through the second half of the twentieth century, the revival was most popularly identified with the crusade evangelism of Billy Graham and his associates.

History records the labors of stellar local pastors. Richard Baxter, Jonathan Edwards, Robert Murray McCheyne, Charles Spurgeon, and George W. Truett were model evangelizing pastors. They were personal and pulpit evangelists. They shared the basic convictions that men and women are lost without Christ and that the gospel is the power of God to save them. They understood the mandate of the Master to evangelize. If we share those convictions, we can take the following action steps.

THE PASTOR AS PERSONAL "SOUL WINNER"

Every pastor should discipline himself to make regular soul-winning visits. In addition, as we come and go about our daily lives, we must be alert to opportunities to make disciples. The following personal disciplines will help a pastor succeed once he gives himself to that task.

1. *Keep a prayer list, and pray for specific lost people by name.* In the United States, the Federal Bureau of Investigation wants to catch all fugitives, but they know that they capture more when they focus on specific individuals. I have found that a "Ten-Most-Wanted List" is useful for evangelism. It is not possible for me to pray faithfully for a thousand or even a hundred lost people, but I can pray faithfully for ten or twenty. You can too. Cultivate that many people with visits and witnessing contacts.

2. *Try to visit by appointment.* There is an advantage to you for the person you are visiting to know why you are coming. If they won't

make an appointment, they are not ready to receive your witness. If they make an appointment and don't keep it, as will sometimes happen, they are not ready to make a commitment. I'm not one to try to slip up and blindside someone with a gospel presentation. The attempt to make the appointment will cause the lost person to think about his or her eternal destiny—at least for the moment.

3. *Sometimes you should visit alone, and sometimes you should go as part of a team.* One-on-one evangelism is better for dealing with some unsaved persons. Jesus was alone with the Samaritan woman at the well and initiated the conversation against all of the cultural norms of His day. His disciples were surprised to find Him talking to her when they returned from her village.

Two-by-two teams have several advantages. The scriptural precedent is that Jesus sent out the twelve in pairs. Later, He sent out seventy others, two by two. One person can pray while the other person witnesses. It is better if only one witness does most of the talking; the unsaved person who thinks that you are "ganging up on him" will raise his defenses. The partner can help in other ways too. For example, I often have seen a Christian wife jump in and defend her spouse, even though she might have requested that the pastor come to talk to her lost husband. While the pastor is trying to get him to see himself as a sinner who needs a Savior, she will say, "He's a good man. He's a good husband and father." That's the time for the prayer partner to take her out to the kitchen. Sometimes a baby or other small child will distract. The partner can help babysit.

Visiting as a team is good on-the-job training for those who lack experience. I will ever be grateful that the church of my youth enlisted me in the "Andrews Club," one kind of outreach plan. When I was sixteen, I was paired with a mature Christian layman to go out on Sunday afternoons. There is nothing like on-the-job training.

The trend now is for teams of three. There are some advantages to this plan. In threes, a husband and wife need not be teamed with each other. Often they make better soul winners if they are not visiting partners.

THE PASTOR AS EVANGELISTIC PREACHER

Some pastors assume that the lost no longer come to church, and they hesitate to preach an evangelistic sermon to the faithful flock. They should do so for two reasons. Not everyone who professes to be a Christian really is; lost church members need to hear the gospel. Also, real believers need to hear the gospel over and over, and we rejoice to hear it if it is well preached.

How does a pastor prepare an evangelistic sermon? We have already devoted two chapters to sermons and preaching, but evangelistic sermons require special considerations. There are ten steps to preparing such a sermon.

1. *Start with an evangelistic aim.* Sermon preparation ordinarily starts with a text. Then you let the aim of the text determine the aim of the sermon. Sometimes a pastor knows that he needs to address a particular need. Then he must go to the Bible and find a text that addresses that need.

Set your evangelistic goal in words on paper. Make it a worthy aim and be specific. Don't write, "I want to preach an evangelistic sermon." Take careful aim: "I want children to understand the way to be saved and to decide for Christ while they can give Him all of their lives." Or, "I want the unconverted church member to realize that Christ's death is his only hope and to flee to Him." Or, "I want the procrastinator to yield to the Spirit's plea and trust Christ now." Whatever goal you set will be tentative until step four, but an evangelistic sermon starts with an evangelistic aim.

2. *Select an evangelistic text.* A pastor needs a "seed file" of many texts on which he is working daily. So, in this stage of preparation, the preacher is not desperately flipping through the pages of Scripture but is prayerfully flipping through his card file or his notebook of evangelistic texts. Spurgeon considered his preparation 90 percent done when he had his text. When asked how to select a sermon text, he told his students, "Cry to God for it." Of course, every stage of preparation should be saturated in prayer, but that's good advice.

3. *Study that text.* Live with it. Analyze it. See what the commentaries

and other reference tools say about it. Don't go to the next step until you can state the central truth of that text in one clear sentence.

4. *Settle on an evangelistic theme that is true to the text.* Here is where the tentative aim you selected in step one becomes fixed. If necessary, modify the earlier goal to fit the text, or select another text that more closely fits the evangelistic aim. The authority of a sermon becomes diluted if the aim of the text does not match the sermon's aim.

5. *Search for and sort sermon support material that enhances the evangelistic aim.* Evangelistic sermons require good illustrations. That means fresh, attractive, and theologically sound stories and analogies. Don't use trite old horse-and-buggy stories. If the text is a narrative, less narrative illustration is needed.

6. *Simmer it for a while.* Pray over it. Wait on the Lord. Take time to let it incubate; a seed needs time to grow. Obviously, such a sermon can't be assembled on Saturday night.

7. *Structure the outline or other plan of organization around the call to faith.* Everything moves toward the evangelistic appeal. The invitation is not an appendix attached to the end of the sermon. That kind of appeal is a relatively recent innovation in preaching. Charles G. Finney, a Congregational evangelist of the mid-nineteenth century, introduced the "anxious bench" in his meetings. He emphasized the importance of public, immediate commitment. Earlier evangelistic preaching made the whole sermon an appeal to trust Christ.

The sermon structure might take one of several forms. H. Grady Davis and others who followed his lead organized the sermons in one of five basic forms: (1) a subject discussed, (2) a thesis supported, (3) a message illumined, (4) a question propounded, and (5) a story told.[3]

8. *Spend some time on sermon style.* A sermon needs to be clear, interesting, and forceful. It is not enough that people understand the preacher. He must labor to make his message so clear that the hearers cannot misunderstand it. If a message is not interesting, the lost will not give attention.

9. *Surrender it all to the sovereign Holy Spirit.* From start to finish, the preparation must be committed to the only One who can empower it. The preacher must surrender himself as well. Edwards said,

"I go out to preach with two propositions in mind. One, every person ought to give his life to Christ. And two, whether or not anyone else does, I will give him mine."

10. *Send it forth for His glory and confident of His blessing.* Think of your sermon as an urgent, special delivery letter to the lost. Don't leave it on your desk. Don't dispatch it so carelessly that it ends up in the dead-letter office. Deliver it with urgency. Isaiah 55:10–11 is a promise of God that will keep a preacher going even when abundant results are not visible:

> As the rain and the snow
>   come down from heaven,
> and do not return to it
>   without watering the earth
> and making it bud and flourish,
>   so that it yields seed for the sower and bread for the eater,
> so is my word that goes out from my mouth:
>   It will not return to me empty,
> but will accomplish what I desire
>   and achieve the purpose for which I sent it.

ORGANIZING THE SUNDAY SCHOOL TO EVANGELIZE

In earlier chapters, we briefly discussed door-to-door evangelism. And we have mentioned, all too briefly, the pastor's role in equipping the church to do evangelistic ministry. Here we can add only a few notes to help a shepherd involve the flock in going after the lost sheep. The Sunday school is a great organization for both reaching and teaching.

1. *Children need special care.* They are at their most impressionable age. Some cautions are in order for working with the little ones. Be cautious about premature attempts to evangelize. As someone said, "Don't pick green fruit." We must be patient laborers in the vineyard. One person plants and another one waters, nurtures, and cultivates. God's own time will come for the harvest. Some people who work

with preschool children push zealously for conversion. We would not question the zeal and love that motives such workers, but how much does a four- or five-year-old child really understand about repentance and faith? How much does such a one fathom about atonement? Caution is the watchword when working with children of any age. We must avoid overly emotional persuasion. It is not kind to frighten children with talk of being left behind when parents and others in the family are taken to heaven. Stoking the fires of hell in pleading with an adult is one thing; terrorizing children is something else.

2. *Youth is a ripe age for evangelism.* The adolescent is part child and part adult. Adolescence is a time of confusion, struggle, and awakening. It is a time of stormy emotions and of physical, mental, and spiritual awakening. God becomes more personal in early adolescence. In middle adolescence, the desire to experience God becomes strong. Later adolescence, with its greater capacity for processing abstract concepts, is a time of sorting out theological beliefs. No wonder most conversions take place in the teen years.

Peer pressure moves teenagers for good or ill. They want desperately to be accepted by their friends or those whom they wish to be their friends. The pastor should be alert to the spiritual needs of youth and guide parents and youth workers in their evangelism.[4]

3. *Adults are reachable too.* Even senior adults need evangelizing. Occasionally, you will see results of a survey showing that most people come to Christ in childhood and youth. Although that is true, these statistics are a bit misleading. Because the poll is never taken with everyone at the end of life, it can report only results of those who have become Christians so far. What is statistically true is that senior adults have a tendency to look back over their life and trust in their good character or good deeds instead of the sacrifice of Christ. This self-satisfaction is a challenge for the evangelistic pastor.

USING THE MASS MEDIA

1. *Radio and television reach many people at once.* They can multiply the church's outreach to the community. Television is very expen-

sive, though. Unless you are running brief commercial ads, the cost of production and airtime tends to prohibit the use of this medium for all but a few churches.

2. *The print media are still very effective for outreach.* If you are in a small town or rural community, the local newspaper will probably be glad for you to write a religion column. If you really want to write, don't rule out the big city daily. When I was a young pastor, I often shared sermon ideas with a pastor friend. One day, I opened the newspaper to see a summary of my sermon printed with my friend's byline. It occurred to me that if the editor thought it was good enough to publish, he might welcome some more. I put together a few sample manuscripts and an idea for a weekly column. I made an appointment with the editor and took them with me. I began writing a weekly column for our metropolitan daily with the title "Midweek Message of the Times." Most of the columns were excerpts or summaries of the previous Sunday's sermon. I focused on a single brief text, gave a narrative illustration, and applied it to life. They were like a gospel tract published in the newspaper, and the paper paid me for the privilege.

3. *Try personal letter writing and direct mail campaigns.* You don't want your message classified as "junk mail," but personal computers today can easily personalize letters. If you are sending one or two hundred at a time, you should further personalize them by a real signature. When preparing for a church evangelistic campaign, a pastor can prepare a letter to each family in the church seeking their involvement. A different kind of letter would go to those on a mailing list of unreached people in the community. A very personal letter could go to those on your prayer list whom you know are unsaved.

4. *The telephone is a wonderful tool for evangelistic outreach.* Unfortunately, telemarketing has made the use of this tool more difficult. The public generally loves to hate the telephone pitchman. I suppose that a church of which I was pastor unwittingly contributed to that perception. A businessman in the church donated an automated calling machine; he had decided that it would not help his business. I put a staff member on that project. Trying to learn how to use it, he recorded a message, set the machine to work one evening, and went

home. Unfortunately, it did not shut down as planned. The next day, we had several calls to the church office complaining about a recorded message from our church waking people up all hours of the night.

Gaines Dobbins related the story of a more successful use of the telephone. A blind man decided to make random calls from his home. When someone answered, he asked with quiet and earnest concern about his or her church affiliation. He also asked if that person might be willing to chat a few minutes about eternal matters. He spoke of the need to know Christ personally. These telephone visits often opened the door for a follow-up letter or visit. The letters included a gospel tract. A Christian witness would make the visit. Rarely, he said, was he rebuffed. He found that people were hungry to talk about moral and spiritual problems to someone who would listen and give a kind and intelligent reply.[5]

SPECIAL SEASONS OF EVANGELISTIC EMPHASIS

The trend for evangelistic meetings is to have fewer and shorter. Once it was common for a church to have two weeks of revival preaching. The first week might be given to getting the church in a state of revival. The next week would concentrate on the unsaved. Revivals were first shortened to eight days, Sunday through Sunday, then one week. Now the trend is toward a four-day meeting—usually Sunday through Wednesday. This trend accommodates the full-time evangelist. He can schedule more meetings. He might have as many meetings as there are Sundays in a month. The evangelists like the trend for several reasons, among them the fact that love offerings are not significantly smaller for a four-day meeting than during a week or eight-day meeting. Church members and pastors like them because the calendar is so full of other activities. Indeed, some pastors promote the "one-day revival."

We use the term *revival* today less precisely than we should. It might be better to distinguish between an evangelistic meeting focused on bringing souls to salvation and a meeting aimed at church renewal. In either case, focus must be on the work of God's Holy Spirit. Finney believed that a revival was human work following cause-and-effect rules precisely like a man planting a crop and reaping a harvest. Spurgeon probably was closer to the truth with his conviction that God does not always come just when we whistle for Him. "Try and whistle for the wind," he said, "and see if it will come."

Should we schedule such meetings? Should we put them on the church calendar and publicize them? Yes, of course, but let us ensure that we pray to the Lord of the harvest and look trustingly to Him who alone can give the increase.

THE PASTOR'S WORLD VISION

The Great Commission calls us to go into all the world. We must guard against the provincialism that narrows our world to the church family and immediate community. What can a pastor do not only to enlarge personal vision but also to help a congregation lift up their eyes?

1. *The pastor must include the lost world in his prayer life.* Do we really care? Do we really believe that people who have never heard the gospel are hopelessly lost? If we do not burn with a compassion for the lost world, we will never lead a church to be missions minded. Too many people pray like the fellow who said, "God bless me and my wife and my son John and his wife—us four, no more. Amen."

2. *He must preach and teach missions.* It is not enough that the church organization includes a ladies' auxiliary that promotes mission offerings. The pastor must lead the whole church to be missions minded.

3. *A pastor must give financially and lead the church to give to support missions.* It might help to have a missionary speaker periodically. Some missionaries are totally dependent on such deputation work. Our church uses a cooperative giving plan that supports the missionaries, without the need for the missionary to spend time and expense raising personal support. Some churches have special seasons of missions emphasis with prayer and sacrificial giving. Others try to make the whole focus of church and ministry reaching the world for Christ. None of these plans will work, however, without the pastor's personal involvement.

4. *A pastor ought also to do missions work and encourage others to go.* Short-term mission assignments can be part of the church calendar of activities. When I served churches in Louisiana, we organized youth mission trips to Mexico and to French-Catholic southern Louisiana. Mission vacation Bible schools were the heart of the trips. The youth trained at home to teach the Bible lessons. They had to learn a list of Spanish words and phrases. They learned gospel songs and choruses in Spanish.

They developed innovative ways to bridge the language gap. One team put a Spanish language gospel tract on a flip chart. Another arranged for a pastor and his wife to tape a puppet script in Spanish. The youth learned to manipulate the puppets in time with the tape. Some of them who had never done door-to-door witnessing at home did so on both sides of the Rio Grande. In the evenings, the youth choir sang in the plazas and gave their personal testimonies. At night, one team took a portable movie projector and screen into a neighborhood and set it up in a vacant lot. A gospel film drama in Spanish drew an amazing response. One of the greatest blessings to those who went was seeing how dramatically God demonstrated the truth of His promise, "And surely I am with you always" (Matt. 28:20).

In our day, doors are also opening for pastors to make short-term mission trips overseas. While this is not so much the case now, for a time after the fall of the Soviet Union, several of the republics, including Russia, welcomed visiting teams of Christian pastors and teachers. Other teams organize to do mission projects in Africa, India, South America—indeed, every continent.

But we must move on to another matter. It is a pastor's special and sacred duty to administer what some people call church sacraments and what others call ordinances.

chapter thirteen

BAPTISM AND THE LORD'S SUPPER

WHEN THE FRANKISH KING CLOVIS was converted to Christianity, his whole army decided to follow their beloved leader in this rite too. He had them march along the riverbank. White-robed priests dipped tree branches into the water and sprinkled them over the advancing ranks while reciting the appropriate baptismal formula.

Hardly anything distinguishes evangelical churches from Roman Catholic tradition more than those sacred ceremonies called "ordinances" or "sacraments." In Roman Catholic thought, the term *sacrament* came to suggest a rite with some degree of saving efficacy. Most evangelicals insist that the ceremonies do not convey grace in themselves but are important symbols.

At the same time, nothing distinguishes evangelicals one from another more than their perspective on these ordinances. Indeed, some evangelicals do not call them ordinances but sacraments, believing that they are a means of grace. The Lord's Supper is also called a sacrament, Eucharist, and mystery.

Is baptism essential to salvation, or is it merely a symbol? Some people insist that the only scriptural mode of baptism is immersion in water. Others defend a tradition of sprinkling or pouring. A touch of irony is that some people who insist on literal wine (not grape juice) and unleavened bread (not crackers) are more flexible on the mode of baptism. Others who would never admit that sprinkling or pouring is baptism are less literal with the sacred symbols of Communion. In this chapter, we will try to be very practical in looking at both baptism and the Lord's Supper. We will not compromise on clear scriptural teaching, but the beginning pastor needs basic how-to-do-it help as well as theological mooring.

BAPTISM

Baptism is a picture of the death, burial, and resurrection of Jesus Christ. It is also a picture of the believer's own death to sin, his putting away of the old life, and his resurrection to a new life in Christ. It is, furthermore, a testimony of our confidence in our future bodily resurrection.

The mode of baptism in the New Testament pattern seems clear. In the account of the conversion of the Ethiopian eunuch, "both Philip and the eunuch went down into the water and Philip baptized him. [Then] they came up out of the water" (Acts 8:38–39). In telling the story of Naaman, the leper, the Greek translation of the Hebrew Bible, called the Septuagint, used the Greek word *baptizo* ("I dip, immerse") to describe Naaman's dipping in the Jordan River. The translators of the King James Bible avoided offending their monarch by retaining the Greek word *baptize* rather than translating it.

Reformers came to their theology of baptism by different roads. Martin Luther retained infant baptism because he wanted to reform the church only as much as Scripture required. John Calvin defended infant baptism on the basis of his covenant theology. He believed that elect children belong to the body of Christ before they are born. Anabaptist reformers, however, insisted that repentance and faith were prerequisites to baptism.

QUALIFYING THE CANDIDATE

From the beginning, let me say that the only experience I have with baptism is the immersion of a believer in water upon his or her profession of faith in Christ as Lord and Savior. I won't presume to instruct those who believe that infusion or sprinkling is appropriate. I will not offer any support for those who practice baptism of infants or of anyone else who has not made a personal commitment to Christ. My understanding of the New Testament, however, does not make baptism a requirement for forgiveness of sins.

In my faith tradition, two important matters must be clarified with each candidate for baptism. First, is he or she trusting Christ alone for salvation and not the water or the ritual? Both adults and children should be able to give a clear testimony of trusting Christ alone for salvation. I am very cautious about baptizing children. I need some assurance that they are not bowing to pressure from parents or peers. I need reasonable assurance that I am not making a proselyte who will be farther from Christ after this ceremony. I question them carefully. I ask them to tell me why they want to be baptized. If they say, "So I can go to heaven," that is a red flag. I sometimes ask, "If you should die before the baptismal service, would you go to heaven or hell?" I don't want to baptize anyone who is trusting anything but the finished work of Christ.

The second matter that the pastor must clarify is whether the candidate is ready for church membership. In most evangelical church traditions, baptism is the door to church membership. Church membership involves not only privileges but also duties. Is the candidate willing to accept the discipline of learning what it means to be a member of the body of Christ? Will he or she seek to live a life that will bring no reproach to Christ or His church?

INSTRUCTING THE CANDIDATE

Although the pastor has been through this rite of passage with many people before, the candidate is making this journey for the first and only time. The physical aspects of baptism by immersion are often a concern. Some people whom you will baptize have never even seen a baptismal service. If they are new to your church, you might consider walking with them to see the baptistry in advance. Then, in the pastor's study, walk them through a baptism as if you were in the water.

I go through the motions with them telling them something like this: "I'll be in the baptistery facing the congregation. You will be coming down the steps on this side. Men and boys have a robing room on this side; ladies and girls are on the other side. Someone will be in the robing room to help you if you need help. When you come down the steps, I will hold out a hand to help you and guide you to where you will stand in front of me and just to my right. (I get them to walk through the motions.) I will hold out my left hand for you to take hold of with both hands. (I help them grasp my forearm just behind the wrist with one hand over and one hand under my forearm.) Then I'll lower you into the water slowly. I will have my right hand at your back to help you if you need any extra help. I will pause just as the water reaches your face. You won't have to remember to hold your breath; you will instinctively take a breath and hold it. Then you will be completely "buried" in the water for just a moment and raised to live a new life. Then I will turn you toward the steps where you came in. Someone will be at the top of the steps to help you with a towel and anything else you need."

I pray with them. I ask God to make the baptism a vivid testimony of their decision to leave the old life of sin and to live for Jesus Christ from this day forward. I pray that their decision for Christ will move someone else to make that choice.

Some pastors prefer to have the candidate fold both arms across the chest in a completely passive manner. That has the advantage of appropriate symbolism of death, burial, and resurrection.

ADMINISTRATION OF BAPTISM

The pastor must take care in the administration of the sacred rite of baptism. He does not want to efface its beauty or at all eclipse its message. Should the candidate for baptism, while in the baptistery, give a testimony of trusting Christ? If they are comfortable doing so, it may be helpful. It should not be coerced. If the person to be baptized has not made a public profession before this moment, he or she should not be there. Also, because so many people are terrified by the prospect of speaking in public, the pastor usually asks, "Is it true that you have turned from sin and self and are trusting Jesus alone to be your Savior?" The "testimony" is usually limited to a lame yes or no confession. Hopefully it is a *yes*. A barely audible answer is hardly a confession of faith. In fact, baptism *is* a confession of faith. It is saying, "Christ died for me and was buried and raised for me. Therefore, I am dead to my old sinful life. I put it away as one would bury a corpse, and I am raised to new life in Christ."

It might be good at the beginning of the baptismal service, before the first candidate comes into the pool, to remind the church about the significance of Christian baptism. We practice immersion because we believe that it is the New Testament pattern. Jesus and John the Baptist went down into the water and came up out of the water. The same with Philip and the Ethiopian official. On another occasion, you might emphasize that we do this in obedience to the Great Commission of Jesus. You might quote Matthew 28:18–20.

What should the pastor say while baptizing? Your tradition may or may not have a prescribed ritual to recite. Over the years, you likely will become comfortable with a fixed Trinitarian formula. For example, while baptizing each candidate, I call the person's name and say, "Sue Smith, upon your public profession of faith in Jesus Christ, and in obedience to His command, I baptize you, my sister, in the name of the Father and of the Son and of the Holy Spirit. Amen." Then, while lowering the candidate into the water, I recite, "Buried with Him by baptism into death [now the candidate is completely underwater] and raised to walk in newness of life" (cf. Rom. 6:4 KJV).

I recall that the pastor of my childhood, while helping the candidate toward the steps leading from the pool, recited Matthew 3:16: "And Jesus, when he was baptized, went up straightway out of the water" (KJV). He had an impressive and dignified ritual in baptizing.

He always ended the service by reciting, "Lord, it is done as thou hast commanded and yet there is room" (cf. Luke 14:22 KJV).

THE BAPTISM COMMITTEE

A baptism committee can be very helpful in assuring that the service moves with fitting dignity. Both men and women should be on this committee; husband-wife teams work very well. They might be assigned a number of duties, including the following:

1. Prepare the baptistery and supplies. How many hours does it take to fill your baptismal pool? How long does it take to warm it to ninety or one hundred degrees? Does a separate pump circulate the water? If so, where is the switch? If the water stands in the baptistery for several days, you must ensure that algae does not begin to multiply. A cup or two of household bleach might be needed. Or you may use swimming pool chemicals.

2. Contact candidates before the scheduled baptismal service. The church office may send a letter with the date, time, and appropriate instructions. Still, someone should make personal contact at least by telephone. The candidate should know what to bring and what will be provided. Most churches provide towels and baptismal robes. The candidate should know to bring a change of street clothes to wear under the robe. White cotton socks might be recommended or provided by the church. Meet the candidate before the service and help to put him or her at ease. Candidates might not know where to find the robing room. They might have other unanswered questions. When do I go to get dressed? Do I need my own hair dryer? Is the water cold?

3. Work with the pastor to ensure a smooth and meaningful ceremony. If several candidates are to be baptized, the pastor might be glad for helpful reminders of the names. You can write the name with a broad-point marking pen on a stick-on label or name tag. Fix it to the left shoulder so that it is clear to the pastor when he needs that reminder.

4. Someone might need to help the pastor into his waders and robe. The pastor should move with minimal delay from the pulpit to the baptistry. For this reason, he will probably use chest-high waders under his robe. He will appreciate help getting into and out of them.

5. *After the baptism, follow up to prepare for the next service.* Empty the baptistery. Ensure that the heater and the circulating pump are off. Ensure that the baptismal robes and towels are laundered and returned promptly. If you send them to the cleaners, don't forget to go back to get them. Ensure that the pastor's waders are dry and hanging without creases. Leave them piled in a corner if you want them to spring a leak the next time the pastor uses them.

6. *Periodically check the baptistery, the heater, and other mechanical equipment.* Keep the baptismal pool clean. Even if you have a competent custodian or janitor, check to ensure that this often-quiet spot is not neglected. You don't want dead crickets and spiders floating around on the surface when you have your next baptism. Unless someone on the committee is competent to make mechanical inspections, ensure that you have professional preventive maintenance. Baptistery heaters are notorious for causing fires.

THE LORD'S SUPPER

The Reformers held differing perspectives on both baptism and the Lord's Supper. Luther and Calvin both held to a sacramental view of the Lord's Table. Both departed from the Roman Catholic view that the Eucharist was an act of sacrifice to God by a priest repeating the Crucifixion. Instead, the Reformers saw Communion as an act by which God gives a sign to man. Huldreych Zwingli was a more radical Reformer, insisting that the Lord's Supper was a memorial supper and symbol, not a sacrament. Some evangelicals today go too far in saying that this sacred ordinance is "mere symbol." It *is* symbol, but it is more than that. It is sacred symbol, but it is even more than that. "Is not the cup of thanksgiving for which we give thanks a participation in the blood of Christ? And is not the bread that we break a participation in the body of Christ?" (1 Cor. 10:16).

When Charles Simeon, the eighteenth-century English pulpit master, started to college, he was godless, worldly, and carefree. When he went from Eton to King's College Cambridge in 1779, he heard a shocking announcement. The provost, in the first week, informed the new students that an ancient college rule "absolutely required" every student to attend a service of Holy Communion. Simeon later confessed, "Conscience told me that Satan was as fit to go there as I; and that if I must go, I must repent and turn to God, unless I chose to eat and drink to my own damnation." He had three weeks to prepare himself. He made himself "quite ill with reading, fasting, and prayer." The Holy Spirit brought him to such conviction of sin that he "frequently looked on the dogs with envy."

The Communion service came and went. Still he had no peace. Then a week or two before Easter, he bought a copy of Thomas Wilson's book *Instructions for the Lord's Supper*. He was arrested by a line in the book to the effect that the Jews knew what they were doing when they transferred their sin to the head of the offering. The thought rushed into his mind, *What? May I transfer all my guilt to Another? Has God provided an offering for me that I may lay my sins on His head? Then, God willing, I will not bear them on my soul one moment longer.* Following is the conclusion of that testimony of his conversion.

> Accordingly, I sought to lay my sins on the sacred head of Jesus, and on Wednesday began to have a hope of mercy; on the Thursday that hope increased; on the Friday and Saturday it became more strong; and on the Sunday morning (Easter Day) I woke early with those words upon my heart and lips "Jesus Christ is risen today! Hallelujah! Hallelujah!" From that hour peace flowed in rich abundance into my soul, and at the Lord's table in our chapel I had the sweetest access to God through my blessed Savior.[1]

PLANNING AND LEADING WORSHIP AT THE LORD'S TABLE

If baptism should be a sacred deed of devotion to Christ, certainly the Lord's Supper should be. We must not let our disdain for hollow ritual lead us to carelessness with holy things. Plan for a worship experience that honors Christ and edifies the worshipers.

1. *Make good use of a Lord's Supper committee.* The pastor will need help to make this time of worship the high and holy hour that it ought to be. The committee should include deacons or elders who also assist in the serving of the bread and the cup. It is the pastor's duty to train the committee in their duties. Someone should be responsible for all of the physical preparation. Will you buy Communion wafers from a church supply or bake your own? Either way, someone must see to it. For the first thousand years of church history, the bread often was a wafflelike wafer baked between two stone or clay bread prints. There is symbolism worth preserving in having a loaf the pastor can break in view of the congregation. For the same reason, if individual serving cups are used, it is well to have a few unfilled so the pastor can pour them from a serving vessel.

2. *Deacons or others who serve should be well prepared.* Each helper should know in advance what his duties are. Let there be no awkward stumbling about. He should know where he will stand and which part of the congregation he will serve. Will a pianist or an organist, or both, provide music during the distribution of the elements? If so, how will they be served? At least for the cup, the server may take it from the tray and place it within easy reach of the instrumentalist. In other traditions, communicants come to the altar to receive the bread and the wine.

3. *Will the pastor include a sermon in the service?* Churches that observe the Lord's Supper at every service certainly include a sermon. The ministry of the Word should be central in Christian worship. But the ordinance is itself a vivid proclamation of the Lord's death: "For whenever you eat this bread and drink this cup, you proclaim the Lord's death until he comes" (cf. 1 Cor. 11:26.) For this reason, it has been my practice sometimes to remind the congregation that they are preaching the sermon in this hour of worship.

4. *Keep a balance between ritual and creative worship. Ritual* is not a dirty word in worship. A fixed tradition can be a meaningful link to our heritage, or a rut from which we can't escape. Every church has

rituals. If you don't think so, try rearranging the order of service. Start with the sermon, then have a song service. Leave off the offering time. You will find yourself facing a very discomfited congregation. Your church probably has a standard way of worship at the Lord's Table too. Still, you can occasionally do things differently.

For example, try a "silent Lord's Supper." Let the people know a week or two ahead that the service will be different. Prepare the musicians to lead congregational singing without announcing the hymn numbers. Omit all announcements. Whatever instructions you need to give the congregation can be printed in an order of service.

Some winter evening, have a candlelight Lord's Supper. It doesn't hurt to return a little of the mystery to the observance. Our church frequently does this as part of New Year's Eve watch night service. I visited a church in New Orleans where some seminary students dramatically presented the Last Supper in costume much like Leonardo de Vinci's famous fresco. One of my favorite ways of celebrating this hour of worship is to read selected Scripture during the passing of the elements. While the bread is distributed, for example, I might read Isaiah 53. When the cup is passed, I would read one of the Gospels' accounts of the Crucifixion.

WHAT FREQUENCY?

Jesus did not tell us how often to observe the Lord's Supper. He did say, "As often as you eat this bread and drink the cup, you proclaim the Lord's death until He comes" (1 Cor. 11:26 NASB). Presbyterians and Baptists usually observe the Lord's Supper monthly or quarterly. Lutherans, Episcopalians, and Disciples of Christ observe the Supper every Lord's Day.

A church that I attended as a child included the observance every Sunday morning. Then, on Sunday evening, they had a time when the minister asked those who were absent from the morning service to stand for Communion. I recall a man standing near me. An elder brought the plate of wafers and a tiny cup to him. It seemed to my eleven-year-old mind that he swigged it down as one taking a dose of medicine. A church must not get so perfunctory in the ritual that the members lose the wonder of the Christ of the Cross.

Other churches observe the Lord's Supper so infrequently that some members might go for years without being in a Communion service. Most churches will find a frequency somewhere between the extremes. Once a year is not often enough. Every time we meet might be too often. Monthly or quarterly observances seem satisfactory to most congregations. Alexander Campbell, a founder of the Christian Church and Disciples of Christ Communions, understood "the breaking of bread" in Acts 2:42 to be a reference to the Lord's Supper and believed that the church should follow this pattern every time they met. In one church, the members told me that the former pastor had refused to plan a Lord's Supper service. He thought that the church was not spiritually fit for one. In that church, in planning the church calendar the first two years, we scheduled six observances annually. Three were Sunday morning services, and three were Sunday evening services.

I recall a sincere old saint in the first church I served as pastor. She came to church regularly, but when we observed the Lord's Supper, she declined to participate. She did not "feel worthy." As best I could, as a nineteen-year-old pastor talking to a faithful member who was old enough to be my grandmother, I explained that none of us is worthy of the sacrifice of Christ. The text speaks of observing the memorial "in a worthy manner." That is, we must understand that it is a memorial of His body and lifeblood sacrificed for us. I don't think she ever distinguished between the adjective *worthy* and the adverb *worthily*.

IS COMMUNION THE WORSHIP FOCUS?

Should Communion be the central focus of the worship service or an appendix added at the end? The answer to this question will depend a lot on the frequency. If we observe the Lord's Supper every week, we will surely need to select Scripture texts other than the few that relate to this memorial. If we observe it only four or five times a year, those services might well be given over completely to the memorial. That seems the wise plan.

A COMMON CUP?

In the typical evangelical church, the custom is to use individual Communion cups. A preacher in rural Ohio is credited with inventing the tiny cups and serving trays in 1893. Sometimes, a pastor symbolically fills the last few empty cups before sending the trays into the congregation. Convenience and a concern for communicable disease have prevailed over historical practice. Few Communions still share the common cup.

Charles Rice is an Episcopal priest who teaches in a Methodist seminary. In the church to which he belongs, the common cup is still the custom. It is also customary for the priest and those assisting him to drink whatever wine remains in the chalice at the end of the Eucharist. This cleansing of the cup, called *ablutions,* ends with pouring a bit of water in the chalice so that the priest can drink the last dregs in the bottom. While there is no intentional symbolism in this manner of cleansing the cup, the priest does make a contact with every member who partakes of that cup. In the early years of the AIDS epidemic, some communicants were declining drinking from the common cup. A bishop in California announced that he would drain the cup at the end of each Eucharist. He considered it an appropriate pastoral act to show solidarity with a troubled diocese and the pastors who served in it. Without a doubt, there is in the common cup a bonding of people one with another and with their pastor. He drinks with them, as Christ did with His disciples, "the cup of mingled joy and sorrow, all leading to great thanksgiving."[2]

WINE OR GRAPE JUICE?

Welch's grape juice began as a business to meet the demand of churches that were conscientiously opposed to alcoholic beverages of any kind. Some people argue that the wine of biblical days was fermented wine, and therefore we should use the same. Or, they argue, at least we may do so if we please. Strong reasons exist, however, for avoiding wine with alcoholic content. The very practical reason is that we do not want to cause anyone to stumble. An alcoholic who takes the least taste of alcoholic beverage likely will fall back into his former life of drunkenness. In addition, the church will never be able to advocate total abstinence if it does not practice it. As for the biblical argument, the case may be made for diluted wine on the Passover Table. There was no refrigeration in Bible times, and the grape harvest was only a brief season of each year. The case cannot be made, however, on the basis of the Greek word for wine. The word *oikos* is used in the New Testament for both wine that is just pressed from the grapes and for wine that makes one drunk.

CLOSED COMMUNION OR OPEN COMMUNION?

Should the church and the minister welcome all believers to participate at the Lord's Table or only those who are members of that local church? Are members of another church of the same denomination allowed? The tradition of the Landmark Baptists insisted that the ordinance be limited to only the members of the local church. Reasons of church discipline gave validity to this position at first. Someone who was out of fellowship with the church for some scandalous offense was excluded from the Table until he or she repented and was restored. Today, church discipline has fallen on hard times, but a few Baptists still hold that it is a local church ordinance and should be limited to that family.

Surely the Lord's Table should welcome all who know the Lord. As a pastor, I did not consider it my duty to include or exclude any believer. I was pleased to find that every congregation I served gladly followed my leadership in this matter. After all, it is the Lord's Table, not the pastor's or even the church's.

Notice, however, that I have drawn a line by saying "believers." Children who do not yet know the Lord should not be served the Supper, just as they should not be baptized. It is a good opportunity to teach them. In the Old Testament Passover, the rituals, so full of symbolism, were meant to provoke questions from the young ones. "When you enter the land that the LORD will give you as he promised, observe this ceremony. And when your children ask you, 'What does this ceremony mean to you?' then tell them, 'It is the Passover sacrifice to the LORD, who passed over the houses of the Israelites in Egypt . . . when he struck down the Egyptians" (Exod. 12:25–27). That was a teachable moment. So it is with the Lord's Supper. Children will ask why they are not included. A discerning parent will be ready to answer.

The next chapter brings us to the supremely vital matter of a pastor's stewardship of time. Besides self-employed persons, who has the privilege that pastors have to set their own schedules? But in that freedom is a snare. We must be self-disciplined souls with a purpose to pursue and a plan to ensure that we follow through. What does it take to exercise that stewardship?

chapter fourteen

THE PASTOR'S STEWARDSHIP OF TIME

VILFREDO PARETO (1848–1923), AN ITALIAN NOBLEMAN and industrialist, won recognition late in life as an economist and a sociologist. He was no friend of democracy, and some people say that he laid the groundwork for fascism. He is remembered today, however, for his studies and observations that led him to formulate in 1895 the "80/20 Principle." He noticed that people seemed to divide into two groups, the 80 percent "trivial many" and the 20 percent "vital few." He argued that 20 percent had most of the money and influence in society. After his observations of Italy, he expanded his study to other societies and believed that the rule applied in every place he studied.

Other scholars have since expanded this rule to other endeavors. Twenty percent of companies in an industry do 80 percent of the business. Eighty percent of any company's business comes from 20 percent of their customers. Eighty percent of automobile accidents are caused by 20 percent of the drivers. Twenty percent of your effort accounts for 80 percent of your progress.

You will often hear that in any church 20 percent of the members do 80 percent of the work and give 80 percent of the money; the 80 percent majority provides the other 20 percent. It might also be true that 20 percent of a pastor's time and energy spent on ministry that really matters produces 80 percent of the eternal value.

Every pastor knows the frustration of work overload. How can any pastor do all that needs to be done? Goal setting and planning helps a pastor keep a productive work schedule. Successful pastors discipline themselves to weekly and daily routines. A number of time-saving tips will make your stewardship of time more fruitful. We consider such tips in this chapter.

HOW CAN ANY PASTOR DO IT ALL?

It was January when I graduated from seminary and moved to my first full-time pastorate. We had an understanding that the next fall I would begin graduate studies. That gave me about eight months to settle into the new pastorate. In the spring, I noticed that the grass at church was growing untrimmed. I called one of the lay leaders and asked who was responsible for tending the church lawn. He said, "I hate to tell you this, but our former pastor made a deal with the church. If we would buy a good power mower, he would keep the church lawn as well as the parsonage."

He was right; that's not what I wanted to hear. I was willing to do my share of the work, although lawn care was never one of my favorite chores. We had to negotiate a new understanding. After that first year, setting priorities became urgent as seminary classes added to pastoral duties. I needed the cooperation of lay leaders. So I devised the following survey and administered it to a gathering of the deacons and their wives. I asked them to assign a time value to each category in one column headed "Hours per week" or another column headed "Hours per day." Following is the survey with the categories as they were grouped.

HOW MUCH TIME SHOULD THE PASTOR SPEND IN EACH OF THESE PER WEEK OR PER DAY?

BIBLE

1. Devotional time reading the Bible?
2. Sermon study in the Bible?
3. General Bible study, such as for teaching?

PRAYER

4. Private communion with the Lord in prayer?
5. Prayer for the community sick, unsaved, and needy?
6. Prayer for church work, such as sermon ideas, and plans?

VISITING

7. Visiting the unsaved?
8. Visiting newcomers and other prospects?
9. Visiting the church members?
10. Visiting the sick and shut-ins?

COUNSELING

11. Counseling new converts?
12. Counseling and teaching other new members?
13. Counseling for personal and family problems?

ADMINISTRATION

14. Church financial planning and promotion?
15. Guiding other church workers, musicians, and teachers?
16. Care of building and grounds, repairs, and yard upkeep?
17. Stenographic work, prospect files, correspondence, etc.?

STUDY

18. Class work in school?
19. Seminary assignments and preparation?
20. General study and reading?

OTHER WORK

21. Secular job?
22. Other? (specify) _____

Looking back over my very unscientific opinion poll, I see that some things are missing. I wonder why I did not mention committee meetings, preparing and leading worship services and prayer meetings, and time at church fellowships and socials. But the survey served the purpose. And what was my purpose? It was mainly to show the key leadership of the church that no pastor could possibly meet all of the expectations of all of the people. Their vision of the pastor's workweek on average exceeded seventy-nine hours. This did not include time for wife and children or any personal recreation. Following is what the most informed leaders in the church said they expected of their pastor.

- *Time in the Bible*, including devotional reading, sermon study, and general Scripture study, should average twenty and a half hours per week. The opinions varied from twelve to thirty-five hours per week.
- *Time in prayer* averaged thirteen hours weekly. The lowest number suggested was one hour daily; the highest was forty-two hours weekly. The one who gave this high figure divided it into two hours per day for each of the three prayer needs suggested. This person gave consistently unrealistic figures in each of the categories. His or her ideal pastor would have a workweek of 138 hours!
- *Time in visiting* of all kinds averaged twenty-four hours weekly.

I was not surprised that the lay leaders in that church thought that was the pastor's main duty. None of the ten answers provided for less that eleven hours each week in knocking on the doors of the unsaved, of other church prospects, of the sick and shut-ins, and general pastoral calling on the membership.
- *Time in counseling* did surprise me. The leaders thought that this category should require very little of their pastor. Under three hours weekly should take care of all kinds of counseling. One person actually entered a zero—no time for counseling family problems, personal problems, new converts, or any other counseling. Others used fractions here.
- *Time in administration* would require even less time. In fact, less than two hours per week should be enough for all four subcategories combined. Most pastors, however, find this category to be their biggest time consumer.
- *Time in study* was near the end of the survey, and maybe some were catching on that they had already used up more hours than any week affords. Or maybe some of them did not want their pastor in seminary. One person entered a zero; four others left it blank. But averaged in with some more realistic apportionments, this category averaged twelve hours weekly.
- *Time in secular work* was the final category. It was added because everyone agreed that the church was not paying anything close to a full-time salary. Then an open-ended question gave opportunity for anyone to add anything they might choose. Seven of the ten respondents gave no answer to this final category, but one person allotted twelve hours per week for a secular job, and another person added ten hours for "miscellaneous" to make this category add four and a half hours to the pastor's work week.

One may draw a number of conclusions from this exercise. Clearly, laymen have diverse opinions as to how their pastor should redeem the time. This sample of church leaders was in general agreement that the pastor's main business was to visit in the community. In my poll, every person allotted more time to this duty than he or she gave to any other category. On the other hand, no one had a clue as to how much demand there was on the pastor's time for counseling. Nor did they have any awareness of the time-draining demand of church administration. My main objective, however, was for them to see that no pastor could do everything that everyone expected.

Many of us who have given our lives to the pastoral ministry can testify to spending sixty or seventy hours a week in church work. No one can do that every week indefinitely. Nor should anyone try. The issue then becomes, What is the best way to allocate the pastor's time, and how can a pastor exercise the discipline to stay the course consistently? Some efficiencies of time use will make us better stewards of our days and hours. Perhaps the foremost lesson for a pastor's stewardship of time is getting organized, which begins with goal setting and planning.

PLANNING AND GOAL SETTING

At a New Year's Eve watch night service, I led the church in a one-hour session of goal setting and personal planning for the new year. Several years later, a senior adult lady told me that the session changed her life. One statement in particular seemed to grip her attention. She reminded me that I had said, "Some people spend more time in planning their vacation than in planning their lives." She could not escape the thought. It was not original to me, and I don't recall now whom I quoted, but it was an epiphany for at least one member. Everyone, especially every pastor, needs to devote time to goal setting and planning that is aimed at reaching carefully chosen objectives.

Have you discovered the one overarching purpose for your life? Why were you born? What is your destiny? Do you agree with the psalmist that you are created for God's glory? Paul wrote of Jesus our Maker, "All things were created by him and for him" (Col. 1:16). What does that mean to you? God created us for Himself. We live to glorify God and to enjoy Him forever. We must remember our cosmic destiny and God's eternal purpose if we want every penultimate goal to be consistent with His eternal plan.

In a helpful forty-day devotional guide titled *The Purpose-Driven Life,* Rick Warren leads us to ask, "What on earth am I here for?" He answers:

> Long before you were conceived by your parents, you were conceived in the mind of God. . . . It is not fate, nor chance, nor luck, nor coincidence that you are breathing at this very moment. You are alive because God wanted to create you! The Bible says, "*The Lord will fulfill his purpose for me*" [Ps. 138:8, emphasis Warren's].[1]

Long-range planning includes prayerful decisions about objectives for lifetime career goals. In my early teen years, my calling to ministry was fixed clearly in mind. I assumed that I would remain a pastor. In time, my plan opened wider. If it would please the Master, I would spend about twenty years in the pastorate and then twenty more in training other pastors and in writing. The final reality was that I remained a pastor for thirty years. One might need to break down career goals into four- or five-year segments. For example, blocks of time are required to finish college, gain a seminary education, serve an apprenticeship, and start a church and see it established. These are segments of a purpose-driven life. You must do more than think about goals; you must write them down.

The Yale class of 1953 was the subject of a well-known twenty-year study. Researchers interviewed the recent graduates about their future plans. Only 3 percent had written goals and plans of action. Twenty years later, the follow-up study found that this 3 percent was happier and more content than the others. In addition, this small group had achieved more and amassed more wealth than any of the remaining 97 percent of their classmates.[2]

Hopefully, a pastor will have a higher aim than mere personal contentment and the accumulation of wealth. Whatever the goals, they should be in writing. If we take aim at a target, we will not hit it every time; if we aim at nothing, however, we are sure to hit it. Some pastors are like the cowboy in a story of a little frontier town. Bull's-eyes were painted on barns, fences, houses, and trees all over town. In the center of every bull's-eye was a bullet hole. When a visitor asked about the expert marksman, he learned that a cowboy had fired the shots, then painted bull's-eyes around wherever the bullets landed.

A logical unit of time for planning is one year. Many people think in terms of New Year's resolutions. That is a start, but a resolution is not a plan. "I resolve to lose fifteen pounds and keep it off." Such resolutions tend to last until the middle of January without more specific how-to planning. Consider setting aside several hours over a period of days for annual planning. Start with one sheet of paper divided into sections for each of several areas as you think appropriate. Some goal categories might be *Spiritual Formation, Family, Finances, Physical Fitness,* and *Pastoral Ministry.* You might use a second page to subdivide the last category. Think about your preaching ministry, pastoral calls, evangelism, and church growth, to name a few. Then, as ideas come to mind, write them down in brainstorming fashion. Don't stop to evaluate each idea as it occurs; just write it down. You will come back later and assign priorities to the goals. You can strike out unrealistic goals for this year and keep them in mind for future years. That is one advantage of considering each goal, even if you cannot imagine reaching it in the year ahead.

For example, perhaps you have a five-year goal for your family to get out of debt. If your debt amounts to about one year's worth of income, you might decide to reduce your debt by 20 percent this year. What bills will you pay first? A student loan at low interest might not be due this year. Your car note might have a very high interest rate amortized over five years. You realize that it is keeping you in bondage to your creditors. Perhaps you will decide to pay that off early.

Jane and Andy were in their first year of ministry after seminary. It had been a financial struggle, with twins arriving before graduation. The church offered a housing allowance instead of a parsonage, but they had to rent until they could save enough for a down payment. They did want to buy a home, though, and settle in the community. This would let the church know that they were not just passing through on the way to a bigger church. Then, whenever God did move them to a new field of service, building equity in a home would give them more to show for their time than just a stack of rent receipts. They set a goal to save $200 per month from the church salary for one year to accumulate $2400 toward a down payment. They planned to add any extra income Andy might earn by outside speaking and weddings. Jane planned to do some babysitting to help pay off their debts. They realized that a mortgage company would be looking at their ability to repay a note; they still had a significant debt load. It took a little longer than they planned, but without a plan they never would have reached their goal.

Pastor Paul was in his fourth year of Bible college when Old First Church called him to their small town. He was still unmarried, but the church thought that he was just what they needed to fill the empty pews in their relatively new sanctuary. He came with a head full of ideas to do just that. He knew that preaching was his greatest strength. At a church growth conference, he heard pastors of super churches talk about the incredible power of television to reach the masses. He decided to start a radio ministry immediately and move to television as soon as the church could afford the start-up expenses. He hoped that would be as soon as graduation in May. Pastor Paul had a great vision, but he was always a little short on specific steps to reach his goals. The church saw a spurt of new interest with the coming of the new pastor, but his dynamic preaching did not fill the sanctuary. Soon, he learned how very expensive it was to get on television and how overburdened the church budget was in paying for the new sanctuary. He became frustrated. By the time he was graduated, he was praying for deliverance from the trap of Old First Church.

Planning and goal setting involve more than vision and long-range objectives. A pastor must also plan in intermediate and immediate time frames. By intermediate, I mean calendar plans for a quarter, a month, and a week. Immediate plans are for each day. Suppose that a pastor sets a goal for his church to see one hundred people accept Christ this year. How many of those will the pastor have to witness to personally? One pastor might decide to make one thousand visits for one hundred decisions. Is that realistic? Can a pastor make twenty presentations to unsaved people each week all yearlong? It would be a rare pastor who could devote one afternoon and evening every week to personal evangelism. Eight or ten soul-winning visits would be extraordinary in that amount of time. Planning will lead a pastor to multiply himself by training others also to be evangelists. Together, they will soon realize that they need help in finding the unsaved and making appointments to visit them. It becomes a team effort.

Planning a church calendar is another matter. Sometime before January, the church should plan and adopt a calendar of activities for the year. Big events, such as Bible conferences, missions focus weeks, vacation Bible school, evangelistic crusades, perhaps a lay renewal weekend, and other activities are spread on the calendar. It might be wise to include a "Christian home week." That week you clear the calendar of all church meetings between Sundays and encourage members to plan evening activities with their families. Our church cancels Sunday evening services as well as Wednesday prayer meeting that week. Also note times when the pastor and other staff members are away, such as for denominational conventions and training events. The calendar has a way of keeping the pastor focused on upcoming events.

A PASTOR'S WEEK

Dr. Gordon Clinard, one of my seminary professors, suggested that a pastor might speak to a civic club on "How I Spend My Time." I have rarely been invited to speak to a civic club, perhaps because I never joined one. Here, however, is a typical week for me as a pastor. Certain things are daily commitments, such as devotional Bible reading and prayer before breakfast. Otherwise, a pastor's agenda moves ever toward Sunday. Plan goals for the week before you plan each day.

Some pastors prefer to take Monday as their day off. Sunday is an intensive day; a physical and psychological dip might occur that whispers the plea for relief. Certainly every pastor needs a designated day of rest. We ought to work six days—that, too, is part of the commandment—but we are human and need the rhythm of one day of rest.

Certainly Sunday is not a restful day for a pastor. I preferred Friday as a day off, but for several years I found Thursday suitable.

If Monday is a workday and if your church has vocational help, it is a good time to have staff meetings. Take an hour or two on Monday morning to gather the secretary, musician, minister of education, youth pastor, and any others on the team. It is a time to seek unity of purpose and to coordinate efforts. Praying and planning together are essential.

The agenda should begin with a Scripture reading and prayer time. A small group that meets for prayer regularly can find real blessing in conversational prayer. Instead of praying around the circle with a series of monologue prayers, teach the team to pray one topic at a time with anyone who wants to talk to the Father about that need, doing so while the item is before the group. That's the way a conversation works. Such prayer might last a while, but it is never a waste of time.[3]

If evangelism is as important to your ministry as it should be, you will spend a while praying for lost persons by name. After prayer time, our custom was to update our "Ten-Most-Wanted List." Every staff member was encouraged to have a personal prayer list of ten people whom they were trying to reach for Christ. We also had a list of ten on whom we agreed to focus together.

After this, you might turn to the church calendar. It is good to focus here on three categories: Looking Back, This Week, and Upcoming Events. You might evaluate yesterday's worship services and discuss what went well and what might be done better. If you had a big event, such as a revival meeting or a lay renewal weekend, it is good to spend time debriefing. Plan also to conserve the results of the big effort. Then turn attention to such big events as are coming in the weeks ahead.[4]

The pastor should make staff assignments appropriate to each person's gifts and calling. As much as possible, you want the staff to volunteer for duties for which they feel responsible. Full-time staff, of course, can carry more of the load than part-time and bivocational workers. Secretaries feel more a part of the professional team if they accept assignments that are not strictly clerical. Everyone on staff should be involved in reaching people for Christ and His church.

Another regular item for the agenda should be church news. Take a few minutes to brainstorm newsworthy happenings among members and others attached to the body in some way. If you publish a weekly newsletter, whether mailed or distributed at church, you should include real news about people in the fellowship. You want your church paper to be more than just a collection of promotional items of upcoming events and a report of nickels and noses counted last week. So put your heads together and think: Who in the church has done something newsworthy in the past week? Recognize yeoman service in the church organizations and activities. Help members keep up with what is going on in the daily world of their fellow members. Someone might have a news item about a member of the church who is on military assignment or at college. If you mail the newsletter to members who are away, they see their names in print and know that they are still a part of the church. It also reminds other people to pray for them. Regardless of whether you publish a newsletter, you should spend time on any news about the whole church that is fit for public consumption.

The newspapers and radio and television stations are always looking for real news items. Most churches send them only promotional copy about things that are to happen. An editor welcomes real news about something out of the ordinary that actually happened. It might be twenty young people who are away on a mission project in a city slum. It might be a child who earned an award for Scripture memorizing or someone who was recognized for twenty-five years of service as the church organist. It is a good idea to spotlight these examples of outstanding accomplishment.

Finally, there might be a time in the staff meeting for any other matters that a staff member thinks warrant time on the agenda. It is important that these be added to the agenda at the beginning of the staff meeting, even if they will be considered last. This serves two useful purposes. First, it keeps staff members from suddenly thinking of something about which they want to talk, although they did not enter the meeting prepared to do so. Second, it alerts the staff at the beginning of the meeting to items that might take some time for discussion. This helps to keep things moving with a minimum of wasted time.

The pastor should spend some of Monday studying and gathering materials for teaching and preaching that week. What will you do at the midweek prayer service? Do you have a class to teach? Do you have texts and at least tentative titles for next Sunday's sermons? The musicians must have these items of information early in the week. So does the secretary if you want them printed in a bulletin or worship guide.

On Monday afternoons, you might have hospital calls to make. Or you might need to call on someone who visited the Sunday services. If you do not have other visits to make, how long has it been since you called on members in the nursing homes and retirement communities?

Tuesday might be a good day for outreach visitation. Those who can make day visits might meet at 10 A.M., receive prepared assignments, pray together, and go out two by two. Some of them might go as evangelism teams. Others might call on recent visitors to the church or those who otherwise expressed interest. Some people might engage in a ministry of encouragement to members who are unable to attend. On Tuesday evenings, another group might gather to go out into the highways and hedges of the community. It is a good idea for the pastor to meet both groups if scheduling allows. As much as possible, take someone with you as your own visiting partner; treat this as an opportunity to train someone in ministry.[5] Pastors' conferences and denominational meetings are often scheduled on Tuesday morning or at noon. Some pastors want to be involved in service clubs or other community activities also.

By Wednesday, Sunday morning's sermon should be taking shape, but two other regular routines require the pastor's time at midweek. I always tried to make hospital calls on Mondays, Wednesdays, and on weekends as needed. Visiting on Wednesday afternoon allowed me to bring an up-to-date report to the praying congregation at our midweek service. Monday mornings seemed to be peak times for the hospital census; doctors and patients alike want to clear out of the hospital if possible before the weekend. Any pastor will have to make some adjustments, depending on variables of the particular pastorate. For instance, if you are in a community that is forty minutes from the nearest hospital, you cannot run to make hospital visits every day.

Emergencies will always disrupt a routine, but there must be a routine. You will have midweek services in the evening, perhaps a church supper and prayer meeting. Are you prepared to lead a prayer meeting with a Bible study or devotional time? One pastor friend who recently retired from Calvary Baptist Church in my hometown always made the midweek service a full song-and-sermon time. He trained his large and growing congregation to bring their unsaved friends. They knew that he would preach the Bible and give an evangelistic appeal. This church consistently baptizes more than one hundred souls every year—sometimes more than two hundred.

Thursday is a day to clear your calendar and your desk of everything but finishing sermons for Sunday. You have read about this procedure in an earlier chapter. At least the Sunday morning sermon should be polished before you leave work on Thursday. The Sunday evening sermon also should be clearly structured by now. It should at least be outlined with some detail. You might find that final preparation for this message comes easier after the morning sermon is finished.

If your day off is not earlier in the week, Friday is one possible time to go fishing, golfing, or whatever else rests and refreshes you. You should also try to keep Saturday clear of church duties. If you have really put in a week of work since last Sunday, people at home need your presence. And like everyone else, the pastor has chores in the house and on the lawn. You spent a week meeting the demands of everyone but your own family; don't come to the end of the week and say, "My own vineyard I have neglected" (Song 1:6).

THE DAILY ROUTINE

The most important planning a pastor does is to set a daily routine. The story of Charles M. Schwab and efficiency expert Ivy Lee is well known. Lee, the consultant, was trying to sell Schwab a training seminar for executives in his brokerage firm. The chief executive was a hard sell. Lee gave him one idea to try. Handing Schwab a blank piece of paper, he instructed him, "Write down the things you have to do tomorrow. Then go back over the list and number them in order of priority. Tomorrow, start on item number one and stick with it until you are done. When you can cross it off your list, go on to item two. Stick with it until you can cross it off, and go on to item three. You might not get through everything on your list, but when the day is done, you will have done the most important things you had to do. At the end of the day, make a new list for the next day. Try that for one month. If you find it helpful, teach your top managers to do the same thing. At the end of two months, send me a check for whatever you think the idea is worth."

Two months later, Schwab sent Lee a check for $25,000. He thought the idea well worth that amount. I could not put a dollar value on that habit in my ministry, but I began to make my daily "to-do list" when I first read that story. It has been a priceless boost to progress.

I had to learn not to shortcut the process. I am tempted to make a list and then pick what I want to work on. The second step, arranging the list in order of priority, is essential. I might not be able to cross off as many items, but I will not spend all of my time on items of secondary and tertiary importance. It feels good, of course, to take a pen and draw a bold line through one more item on the list. Beware the temptation to pick the quick, easy, and more enjoyable chores. Stick to the real order of priority.

A college professor demonstrated the importance of this principle of time management with an object lesson. He filled a bucket with a dozen fist-sized rocks and asked the class: "Is the bucket full?" They agreed that it was. "Are you sure?" he asked as he took a bag of gravel and emptied it into the pail. "And now is the bucket full?"

"Maybe," said a few cautious students. The professor then took a bag of sand and poured it in, shaking it down as he added it to the rocks and gravel.

"Now is the bucket full?"

"No," answered the students. The professor then added a big bottle of water until the liquid brimmed over. All agreed the bucket was now full.

"What is the point of this demonstration?" asked the professor.

A student raised his hand. "It is to show that even if you think your schedule is full, you can still add to it."

"No," answered the professor, "I only wanted to remind you that unless you put your big chores into the day first, you will never get them in later."[6]

SEVEN TIME-SAVING TIPS FOR THE PASTOR

Every productive pastor develops his own habits of efficiency. Following are some tips that have served me well.

1. Plan your preaching in large blocks. One of the biggest time-wasting mistakes of the beginning pastor is to start Monday with no idea what he will preach the next Sunday. Tension builds to desperation level by Saturday night. That is unnecessary.

M. E. Dodd was a well-known Baptist pastor of the first half of the twentieth century. He was at the same time a pioneer radio preacher, deeply involved in denominational service, mission work, Christian education, writing, and speaking in churches and conferences across America and around the world. I made the purpose of my research and writing for a doctoral dissertation to find out how he could do all of these things and still come to the pulpit week after week with fresh and vital exposition. I drew several conclusions from my study but none more revealing than that Dodd mastered the art of long-range planning for the pulpit. He planned his pulpit work a year in advance. He specialized in preaching sermons in series: doctrinal studies; biographical studies, such as a series on the life of Christ; practical themes; and especially expositions through Bible books.

In his expositions, he would select the books on which he planned to concentrate the next year, perhaps preaching twenty-six sermons through John's gospel on thirteen Sunday mornings and evenings. If he were planning to preach through an Old Testament book, he might write a letter to an imminent Old Testament scholar such as John R. Sampey in Louisville and ask him to recommend books and commentaries on that Bible book. If it were a New Testament book, he might write A. T. Robertson in Fort Worth for suggestions. After he studied enough to decide on texts and topics, he had them printed with the dates on which he would preach them. This publicity in newspapers and leaflets became a promise to his congregation, but it also was a prod to the preacher, keeping him focused on his preparation. He wasted no more time searching for a text or a sermon idea.[7]

2. *Answer mail immediately or not at all.* Don't open your mail until you have time to answer it. Discipline yourself to handle each piece of paper one time. If it is junk mail, you should feel no guilt about throwing it away unopened. That applies to e-mail also. Even items from friends might be deleted unopened if they are marked "Fwd: Fwd." Personal mail you can answer with a handwritten note in the margins. Then take the original with your note on it to the copy machine. Make a copy for your files, and return the original with your answer on it. Even if you have a secretary, save typing or word processing for messages that really need it. In my childhood and youth, it was a big deal to get a typed letter. Then along came mass mailing with printed signatures that looked real and personal. No one is fooled today by those mailings, even if it has colored underlining and "handwritten" marginal notes. Today, we appreciate the truly handwritten letter.

I resisted getting a fax machine but don't see how I could manage now without one. They save time over writing a letter and mailing it, but the big time-saving is in instant delivery. E-mail and Internet instant messaging can also be great time-savers if we do not let ourselves chat away on matters of little importance.

3. *Use drive time wisely.* Depending on how much commuting you do, drive time can be either a big waste of time or a huge blessing. The average car owner sits behind the wheel five hundred to one thousand hours each year. Check how many miles you drove last year and figure your own drive time. Suppose that you drive fifteen thousand miles a year, half highway miles and half in town. That is probably 150 hours on the highway and maybe 400 hours driving in town. That is fifty or sixty ten-hour days annually. Other than getting from place to place, what are you doing with that time?

You could use some of the time listening to teaching tapes or sermons of outstanding preachers. From Bible societies and publishers, you can get Scriptures narrated by outstanding oral interpreters. A clip can hold Scripture memory cards. On long drives, you might make good use of a cassette recorder to dictate letters for a secretary to transcribe. Even if you are your own secretary, it is good to compose your thoughts in advance. Record flashes of inspiration or seed thoughts that come as you drive. A road sign or bumper sticker might make a good sermon illustration.

I remember once driving through Baton Rouge, Louisiana, and passing a pickup truck with a boy about eight years old between a crew-cut dad and young mother. The bumper sticker read, "My son can whip your honor roll student." I chuckled and took note; it might pop up in a sermon some day, or not. At least it sharpened my observation skills.

Now that practically everyone has a cell phone, many of your contacts can be made while you are on your way from home to the office, hospitals, and other meetings. If your state does not already require drivers to have hands-free installation, you should require it of yourself. Also, in heavy traffic you should give your full attention to driving. It is presumptuous to risk your life and limbs and the health of others around you on the road.

If you live and work in an urban area, especially the Eastern corridor from Boston to Washington, you probably use public transit. You have the advantage of reading and doing other work while riding public transportation. Kenneth Taylor began his paraphrase of the New Testament while riding Amtrak to and from work. It was a project for his own family worship so his children could understand the Scriptures. It grew into a very useful published project that recently was revised to make it more a true translation. Some of us in the South marvel that our city cousins get along quite well without owning even one automobile.

4. *Sharpen your skills in coping with the unscheduled drop-in.* Some drop-ins are just being friendly to the pastor; others are really hurting and don't know how to get to the point. You don't want to brush off either type or give offense. Nonetheless, you don't have just to grin (or grimace) and bear it.

A member pops in your door and asks, "Are you busy?" What do you say?

You might say with a smile, "Sure, I'm always busy, but never too busy for you. Come on in. What's on your mind?" Or you might say, "I'm just about to leave to go make a few hospital calls. Do you have time to ride with me? We can visit on the way there. I'll have you back in ninety minutes or so."

Sometimes it will be someone who really needs time with the pastor as a counselor. You might already know the need and that it will take more time than you can possibly give at the moment. You could say, "Come in and close the door. I've been hoping you would come by. I want to pray with you, and then let's look at my appointment book and see when we can have an hour uninterrupted." Then kneel and pray for God's grace in your friend's trial. When you rise, open your calendar and find an agreeable time to meet. When you open the door, encourage the person with a warm handshake or an appropriate hug, depending on the age and sex of both you and the visitor. This is not to say that a pastor should be a workaholic. Nor do we suggest that a pastor never lay aside his scheduled task to deal with an unexpected visitor. Sometimes that is precisely the thing to do.

The perennial time waster is another matter. It might be an active layman recently retired with too much idle time. He thinks that you, too, have little to do, so he often walks in and takes a seat in your study. After a few of these unscheduled interruptions with no true purpose to the conversations, you will dread to see him coming. What can you do to help your brother without letting him destroy your schedule? You might pray about an extra job or two around the church to give him new purpose in life. Maybe he can help with Monday's counting committee, Tuesday's church newsletter, Wednesday's fellowship supper, Thursday's outreach visitation, or Friday's last-minute arrangements of Sunday school records, hymnals, and bulletins. Remember the idle workmen in the marketplace in one of our Lord's parables. Why were they idle? Because no one had enlisted them.

5. *Find out where time is going, and plug the leaks.* Keep a daily log of time use in a notebook for a week. Record everything and how much time it takes. You might be surprised how much time is wasted. It will help you set a definite limit for yourself on things such as

reading daily newspapers and viewing television. Do you have sit-down meals with your family? Do so as often as you can. My wife and I have different schedules for breakfast, so I use breakfast time to scan the daily newspaper. Many years ago, I discovered that I was spending an hour with the morning paper. That's too much. I decided to skip the sports section and the classifieds. Another pastor might prefer to skip the comics and the national news. By listening to news in drive time on the radio or on television at night, one can scan the news lightly. I find myself clipping a lot of articles from newspapers and newsmagazines.

If you keep a TV log, you might be shocked at how much time you are spending there. Plan your television time to avoid wasted time as well as brain drain. Most TV is not worth the time. Too many of us use it only as a diversion from the press and stress of the day. I have tried videotaping programs that I want to see so I can skip commercials that take about twenty minutes of every hour. Fast-forwarding and rewinding, however, eats up about half of that time saved. Television can be a blessing if used wisely. The public library probably has a good collection of family movies to watch without commercial interruption.

I remember a man in the rural village I served as weekend pastor while I was in seminary. Like his neighbors, he was a cotton farmer. Like them, he stopped by the store across the road from the church regularly. And also like many of them, he stayed for a game of dominoes frequently. Unfortunately, unlike his hardworking neighbors, he stayed and played hour after hour with whomever was available. His cotton crop went to weeds and pests year after year. He was the only man in the community without an indoor bathroom in the 1960s. I know pastors who have played golf while family, ministry, and the rest of life went down the tubes.

At the end of the day, perhaps when making the *To-Do List* for tomorrow, look back over the day and ask if you have been a good steward of the time. The Roman general Titus, who conquered Jerusalem in A.D. 70, had the habit of asking himself every evening, "Did I make good use of my time?" We think of siege time as mainly waiting. Not

Titus. No wonder he became Emperor Titus, the one who built the Coliseum in Rome.

6. *Prayerfully plan the day in blocks of time to minimize disruption.* One pastor friend thinks that unplanned drifting is more conducive to trusting the Holy Spirit for moment-by-moment guidance. But prayerful planning is laying our day before God in advance. We ask for direction from the One who knows the future and then move through each day sensitive to the Spirit's right to revise and correct our impression of divine leadership.

Some theologians today talk of open theism or the "openness of God." They mean that even God does not know what is going to happen tomorrow; it depends on free choices that His creatures make today. Evangelical theology sees the whole future as open to a God who is indeed sovereign over all. We don't make our plans and then ask God to bless them; we seek His face and submit ourselves to His will. This goes a long way toward avoiding frustration.

Still, it is unnecessary to turn from studies or other projects every time the phone rings. A secretary or a spouse can answer the phone and take a message. If not, an answering machine or service of your local telephone company can take messages. To get an idea of how much time you spend on the telephone, keep a telephone log for a few days. The necessary calls should be listed and made in one block of time as much as possible, as should calls to return.

Plan a two- or three-hour block of time for visiting the unreached. When calling, make arrangements to visit in one area as much as possible to avoid wasting outreach time with driving and doubling back. Learn to handle the frustration of work overload by thinking incrementally. Usually it is unnecessary to do the whole task in one day. How do you eat an elephant? One bite at a time:

> Inch by inch, life's a cinch;
> Yard by yard, it's hard.

7. *Share the ministry.* Getting things done might begin for some pastors with deciding what things to leave undone and what things to

leave for others to do. Does God put on anyone more responsibility than that person can carry? If not, what is going on with this problem of overloaded pastors? Could they be trying to do more than God wants them to do? But it *all* must be done. It is *all* vital ministry. Yes, but the pastor does not have to do it *all alone*.

Consider these two ways to share the ministry. First, the pastor's task, Paul tells us, is not to do all of the work of the ministry but "to prepare God's people for works of service" (Eph. 4:12). In this way, the body of Christ will be built up and move toward the oneness and spiritual maturity and full knowledge of the Son of God that leads to the perfect ideal of a mature church. As Christ is perfectly mature, so in this sharing of ministry the church will move from infantile weakness to adult strength.

Second, a pastor must learn to delegate. You might enjoy doing the work yourself too much for your own good and for the good of the church. Acts 6 makes clear that delegation and division of labor are within God's plan. This text also gives some guidance on how to share the load. First, decide what should be delegated, perhaps by noticing what work is being neglected. Second, choose carefully and prayerfully the person or persons to match the task. Interestingly, when the Grecian Jews in the church complained that their widows were neglected, the church selected seven men with Greek names to meet the need (Acts 6:1, 5). Third, give specific instructions. Fourth, keep the lines of communication open.

Fifth, in delegating, allow people to do the job without looking over their shoulders. Sixth, that means allowing for mistakes. They might not do it exactly as you would. Is that okay? Seventh, recognize a job well done. The record shows that this event marked a surge of growth in the church (Acts 6:7).

In addition, consider whether your church should have more than one pastor. "But we are too small for more than one pastor," you say. Maybe. Maybe not. In many places, retired ministers, ministerial students, and bivocational ministers would love to share the ministry. In many cases, salary is not an issue with them. More importantly, consider the Scriptures. The New Testament pattern is a plurality of elders, or presbyters, in every local church. In fact, with the possible exception of the letters to the seven churches of Asia Minor in the Revelation, in which some scholars consider "the angel" of the church to suggest a solitary pastor, I do not find an example of any church having only one pastor.[8]

We have emphasized ways for the pastor to increase his efficiency as a good steward of his few days on this earth. Lest you despair of the task, remember that work was a part of God's original plan in Creation. It is not, as some people suppose, a curse that came on mankind with the sin of Adam and Eve. Productive labor is a blessing that came in the original order of Creation. "The LORD God took the man and put him in the Garden of Eden to work it and take care of it" (Gen. 2:15). The disobedience brought the curse that turned satisfying work into "painful toil" (3:17). In Christ, we are redeemed, and we anticipate the promised redemption of the whole fallen cosmos. Have you learned something in this chapter that will make your labor more productive and satisfying? Then take to heart the point of the following story.

A stranger to America visited one of our large and frenetic cities. Everyone seemed to be ever in a hurry, and no one seemed to be at peace. On a certain day, she was to go to an appointment five miles across the metropolis. She planned forty minutes by taxi to make the trip. But, as she started out, her American host pointed out that the subway would take her within two short blocks of her destination at a considerable savings of time and money. They made the quick trip together. As they came out into the sunlight at the destination, the American host missed his guest and looked back to see her sitting on a bench at the subway exit. He hurried back with some alarm to see what the problem was. "No problem," answered the stranger to American ways, "we have saved twenty minutes. Now we can stop and enjoy the sights and sounds of this place."

chapter fifteen

THE PASTOR'S PERSONAL LIFE

THOMAS CHALMERS BECAME PASTOR OF rural Kilmany Church in Scotland in 1793 at age twenty-three. Scotland has a rich heritage of great preachers, but in this first charge, Chalmers was not a great preacher or pastor. For seven fruitless years, he struggled, feeling dry, dusty, and powerless. He stumbled on in this parish until a series of providential events led him to discover the cause of his spiritual poverty: He was lost. He came to the Savior and preached ever after with a holy passion, one of Scotland's best. He is remembered today by his most famous sermon: "The Expulsive Power of a New Affection." In that sermon, based on 1 John 2:15, he insists that the way to disengage the heart from the love of the worthless world is to fix the affections on the excellence of the heavenly Father.

This chapter draws the attention of the pastor to very personal matters, including matters of the heart. In the providence of God, might someone read this far without settling the question of who will be Lord of his life? If so, he would not be the first pastor to try to do the work of God without the power of God. Before reading another page, consider the claim of Christ on your life; He died for you. He took your sins in His sinless body to the Cross. When He came out of that borrowed tomb, He left your sins in the grave. Why should you try to deal with them any other way? If you have not found peace with God, run now to Jesus, the Prince of Peace. Then, when that priority issue is settled, you must heed some other things as a pastor.

DON'T NEGLECT FAMILY MATTERS

The pastor's family must be a priority. Take your day off. Take time for your wife and children. Take vacations, even if it is just tent camping in a state park. You are your wife's pastor, but first you are her husband. You don't have to be her pastor, but you must be her best friend, lover, and life companion. Your children also need a father first and then a pastor.

I have a friend whose wife decided to join a church of a different denomination. I think that arrangement has worked well. I notice also that in the black Baptist tradition, both the pastor and his wife are usually members of a church other than the one he serves. A friend in that tradition told me of a time when his wife was not happy being a pastor's wife. Fortunately, they had a pastor to whom they could go, and they did. Their pastor recommended that she come and sit under his ministry for a few weeks. Because he was her pastor, the church her husband served had no problem with that arrangment.

Spend time with your children while they are children. When my two children were small, I was often preoccupied with church work and finishing a Th.D. degree. For several months while writing my dissertation, I wrote at night while they slept. I slept until noon and had a little free time in the afternoons. I promised myself that I was going to give them priority time when this push was past. The time came. I put an evening on the calendar in early summer for my nine-year-old son. We took a walk in the woods. It was a leisurely stroll, and we had a good father-son visit. Early the next morning at the office, I discovered that I had missed a deacons' meeting. Now that my children are grown, I wish that I had missed more deacons' meetings!

BEWARE FAILURE IN FINANCIAL MATTERS

The pastor is subject to a temptation that afflicts virtually everyone else in our affluent culture—the illusion that money can buy happiness.

A recent study in the *Journal of Personality and Social Psychology* reported that even $150,000 was not enough salary if others could afford better things.[1]

1. *Live within your income and guard your credit rating.* It has been well said, "If your income does not keep up with your out-go, your upkeep will be your downfall." Businessmen do not like deadbeats. They especially dislike deadbeat pastors. Anyone can make a mistake in budget planning. Young couples frequently fail to plan for unexpected expenses. The unexpected expense does come, usually a significant one every month. If you let one catch you unprepared, go immediately to your creditors. Explain your crisis and work out a schedule of regular payments. Even a small payment, if regular, can save your reputation. Those who try to hide from their creditors have no excuse and no hope. "And you may be sure that your sin will find you out" (Num. 32:23b). The reputation of a pastor who does not pay his bills follows him. Then it will go before him and limit opportunities in ministry.

As a rule, don't buy depreciating assets on credit. That includes automobiles. What makes you think that you must have a new car and five years of car notes? You might wear it out before you pay it off. A house that might be worth 5 or 6 percent more a year from now is worth buying on credit. Few home owners would ever accumulate the price of a house while paying 20 percent to 25 percent of their income for rent. The sad truth for most young couples is that they do not have the discipline to accumulate a down payment. Get out of debt.

2. *Plan and work for financial security.* What some ministers consider trusting God might instead be a sad case of spiritual presumption. In the wilderness temptation, Satan tempted Christ to jump from the pinnacle of the temple. Wouldn't that be a masterful display of faith? After all, popular messianic expectation called for Messiah suddenly to appear in His temple. The people rather expected Messiah to come floating down from above. But Jesus knew the difference between faith and presumption. Some pastors do not.

I knew a young couple who wrote checks "on faith." They expected God to provide the money for a deposit to cover the check before it got to the bank. This practice is also called writing "hot checks"; it is a crime. I also knew a seminary student whose small children went barefoot in winter. He said that he had prayed about a decision to buy an expensive television console. God did not tell him not to, so he concluded that it was the will of God.

Read Proverbs. Billy Graham recommends that every Christian read one chapter every day. Thirty chapters make it convenient to go through the book each month. The Proverbs are not written to teach us how to be rich but how to be honest, just, and fair (Prov. 1:3). Still, they are full of practical financial wisdom. That includes helping others (3:27), but it does not mean cosigning anyone's note (6:1–5). Work hard to earn your way; being lazy will make you poor (10:5). And remember that riches will do you no good on the day you face death (11:4). Save but don't hoard. Hoarding, after all, is foolish in an inflationary economy (6:6–8; 11:24–25). Be diligent and skillful in the management of money. Plan and budget, but realize that God has veto power over any of your plans (19:21; 20:18). These truths are but a small sample of the financial wisdom that runs through the whole book of Proverbs.

If you are not able to balance your budget, ask yourself some questions. Am I spending presumptuously? Does the Lord want me to turn aside and make a few tents, as Paul did when his financial support lagged?

Should the pastor live in a parsonage or have his own home? The church might not offer the option. If you do have the choice, start building your own equity. My childhood pastor, T. C. Pennell, served our church for nearly his whole career. And he served well. I don't know how well we paid him, but he should have been paid twice as much. He suddenly had a heart attack and died in the pulpit one Sunday morning just as he was beginning his sermon. Soon, the church had to decide whether to ask the widow to vacate the parsonage.[2]

A PASTOR SHOULD HAVE A STRONG WORK ETHIC

A pastor could work twenty-four hours a day seven days a week and not get all his work done. Sermons, soul winning, counseling, caring for the flock, administration of the church, denominational work, and community concerns all clamor for the pastor's time and attention. The temptation might be to despair or to spend time on duties that seem less like labor. Most ministers have no clock to punch. The opportunity exists for a pastor with a lazy streak in him to take advantage of that fact. We are self-supervised for the most part, setting our own schedules and coming and going as we decide.

When John Henry Jowett was a young pastor, he would be awakened early by the clomping of work shoes going past his window. The mills started work at six o'clock. He said, "The sound of clogs fetched me out of bed and took me to my work." He advised ministers, "Enter your study at an appointed hour, and let that hour be as early as the earliest of your business men goes to his office."[3]

It boggles the mind how a John Calvin, a John Wesley, or a George Whitefield could preach every day, sometimes several times a day, and still study, write, organize, and promote a mighty movement of men and nations. They did not do it at their leisure. They worked at it. If a pastor is tempted to drift from duty to duty without plan or urgency, let him consider such admonitions as Proverbs 6:6a (cf. vv. 6–11): "Go to the ant, you sluggard."

A PASTOR MUST BE A READER

Television is no substitute for reading. Turn it off and open a good book. If you are addicted to TV, let me suggest a verse of Scripture that you might consider printing on a card and posting on your set: "Turn my eyes away from worthless things; preserve my life according to your word" (Ps. 119:37).

1. *Read the Christian classics.* Spurgeon read John Bunyan one hundred times. Most pastors today have never read him once. *The Pilgrim's Progress* is one of the greatest works in Christian literature, but it is also a classic of English literature. If a pastor missed all of the spiritual message in that allegory, which would be impossible, he would still be enriched by the exercise. The vivid Anglo-Saxon words speak to people. Maybe he would quit using so many words of Latin origin in his sermons.

Richard Baxter's *The Reformed Pastor,* first published in 1656, is another true classic worthy of every pastor's reading. The term *reformed* in the title speaks more of a Puritan pastor's spiritual reformation than of that particular set of Calvinistic doctrines that we think of today when we use the term.

2. Build a library. Be selective. Here is a good rule: Borrow from the library instead of buying a book you will read only once straight through and probably never open again. Take notes that you might need for sermon illustrations and as memory joggers. Make a habit of summarizing library books in two to five pages. In my early years, I took thousands of notes on four-by-six-inch index cards. Now it works well for me to summarize a book on the word processor. If it is a Bible reference book or a commentary that you will consult repeatedly, consider buying it. Also, accumulate books in a field of your specialty, such as preaching or pastoral care.

3. Some pastors practice the discipline of reading a book at one sitting. Some notable pastors have made such reading a habit. James M. Gray, G. Campbell Morgan, W. Graham Scroggie, and Ralph Turnbull were outstanding expositors who trained themselves to read a book through before putting it down. Somehow they guarded their reading time against interruptions. Get away from telephone and doorbell for this kind of reading if you can.

4. Learn speed-reading. You might have opportunity to enroll in a speed-reading course, but plenty of good books on speed-reading are available. Check the library as well as bookstores. Speed-reading can increase both your speed and comprehension dramatically. I have to remind myself sometimes to move along since my regular habit is to read with a marking pen in hand.

GIVE MAJOR ATTENTION TO SPIRITUAL FORMATION

What if the physician of souls is spiritually anemic? Can he hope to keep a healthy congregation? Unless the pastor is ever moving toward maturity in Christ, those under his care will suffer loss. Growing in grace is a process of God's grace, not our works. Nevertheless, certain spiritual disciplines nurture the spiritual life.

1. The Word of God is the foremost means of spiritual development. Every pastor needs a daily discipline of devotional Bible reading, serious Bible study, and Scripture memorization. God took the new nation of Israel through the wilderness for a purpose. He wanted to humble them and cause them to hunger. Then he could feed them with manna. This taught them "that man does not live on bread alone but on every word that comes from the mouth of the LORD" (Deut. 8:3b). We, too, find soul nourishment in the same sacred Word. "Like newborn babies, crave pure spiritual milk, so that by it you may grow up in your salvation" (1 Peter 2:2).

Some pastors read the Bible through from Genesis to Revelation every year. A pastor needs a definite plan of daily Bible reading. This may involve reading a certain number of chapters daily, but a better plan would be to read a minimum number of pages. A translation may have a thousand pages of Old Testament and about 350 pages of New Testament. Four pages a day will cover both testaments in one year. Five pages a day will accomplish it in nine months. Six months is too long to go without reading the New Testament, so intersperse a gospel or an epistle while reading the Law and the Prophets. For example, after reading Joshua, you might read Ephesians.

More than read, the Word must be studied. Take notes. Read commentaries. Analyze and assimilate. A pastor must have a discipline of lifelong Bible study.

Memorizing Scripture should also be a regular discipline. The psalmist sang, "I have hidden your word in my heart that I might not sin against you" (Ps. 119:11). Navigators, Campus Crusade, and other parachurch ministries have successful Scripture memorization programs.

2. Make your devotional discipline a top priority. Let the pastor take seriously the call to prayer. Reserve regular top-quality time for the Word and prayer. Jesus sometimes got up a great while before daybreak to go out into a quite place and spend time with the Father. Sometimes He prayed all night. If *He* needed prayer, how much more do *we!* A pastor should periodically set a time for a prayer retreat. Sometimes it might be with a prayer partner or a small group. At other times, let the pastor be alone with his Master. Fasting is a discipline of value that goes with prayer, although you shouldn't make a show of it or any other devotional exercise.

Some people who read these lines will already be involved in a busy pastorate. Someone might object, "I wish I *could* get away to pray, but the demands of the job do not allow it." One evening in Capernaum, Jesus was overloaded with demands of ministry, healing, and exorcisms. The next morning, He got up a great while before day and slipped away to a deserted place. There, He talked to the Father (Mark 1:35). At daylight, Peter and some other disciples pursued Him until they found Him. Peter said, as if to rebuke the Master, "Everyone is looking for you!" (vv. 36–37). In other words, "What do You mean slipping off like that? The crowds are already gathering." Jesus did not let the demanding multitudes set His agenda. He did not tell Peter, "Go tell the people that I will be right there." Instead, He responded, "Let us go somewhere else—to the nearby villages—so I can preach there also. That is why I have come" (v. 38).

3. A pastor must live a Spirit-controlled life. A lot of confusion exists about the doctrine of the Holy Spirit. Especially needed is a clear word on the teaching about "the baptism" and being "Spirit filled." Everyone agrees that a pastor should be "Spirit filled," but what does that mean?

Much of the confusion will dissipate when we understand that the New Testament writers use a variety of terms to speak of one spiritual reality. Luke has much to say about the Holy Spirit in his gospel and Acts. In the first chapter of Acts, Jesus commanded His chosen men to "wait for *the gift*" and used the phrase "be *baptized* with the Holy Spirit" (Acts 1:5b). That promise is fulfilled in the next chapter, where we are told that all of them were "*filled* with the Holy Spirit" (2:4). The terms *gift, baptism,* and *filling* surely refer to the same event. The apostle Paul also used a variety of terms. In Romans 8:9a, the believer is "*controlled* by the Spirit." In Galatians 5:16, we "*live* by the Spirit." In Ephesians 5:18, Paul again speaks of being "*filled* with the Spirit." This is not to say that no differences exist among these words. Each, of course, has its own meaning. But hairsplitting distinctions in the terminology leads to a rending of fellowship in the body of Christ. Certainly, if one had to choose between sorting out the terminology and having the experience right, it should be no contest. How does a pastor ensure that he is rightly related to God the Holy Spirit?

Let us assert that we are seeking a Person, not an experience, however great and blessed spiritually it may be. We are seeking God the Holy Spirit. The Scriptures never call us to seek an experience, but we are often called to seek God. And we have His promise many times over that those who seek Him, find Him (e.g., Deut. 4:29–31; 1 Chron. 28:9; Isa. 55:6; Matt. 7:7; Heb. 11:6). Neither are we seeking to gain control of divine power but are seeking to come under divine control. Simon the sorcerer thought that the Holy Spirit was a commodity that he could attain to give him supernatural power (Acts 8:9–24). In Paul's great chapter on the Spirit, Romans 8, he says, "You, however, are controlled not by the sinful nature but by the Spirit, if the Spirit of God lives in you. And if anyone does not have the Spirit of Christ, he does not belong to Christ" (v. 9).

It is entirely possible, of course, for a person to be a Christian and not realize that the Holy Spirit lives within. I once bought a house in a community on the intercostal waterway of south Louisiana. The man who sold it to me told me a lot with a dock and a boat slip belonged to the community. He said that he had never joined the club, however, and did not know how much it cost. I asked a neighbor about it and found that ownership in the common lot was the right of any property owner in the community. He gave me a key, and we enjoyed the benefit, fishing and crabbing on the dock. The former owner had a possession that he never realized.

Third, although this blessed benefit of being under the Spirit's control is our birthright as believers, we have plenty of urging in Scripture to be diligent in seeking the Spirit. Jesus said, "Ask and it will be given to you; seek and you will find; knock and the door will be opened to you" (Luke 11:9). "If you then, though you are evil, know how to give good gifts to your children, how much more will your Father in heaven give the Holy Spirit to those who ask him!" (v. 13).

Fourth, once a pastor comes under Holy Spirit control, he must take care to continue in that place. We must let no sin take root in our life that will grieve the Spirit (see Eph. 4:30). We must avoid the self-assertion that resists the Spirit (Acts 7:51) or puts out the Spirit's fire in our souls (1 Thess. 5:19). Remember that He is the Spirit of holiness; we must serve Him in holiness (Luke 1:74–75). "Above all else, guard your heart, for it is the wellspring of life" (Prov. 4:23). Every fall of a notable television personality or other well-known minister stands as warning. Just when we think that we are standing firm, the enemy comes to trip us and make us fall. It might be jealousy of another minister, covetousness, or pride. We might be impatient with the weakness or wickedness of those we want to lift. We all have feet of clay. We all must take care, trusting not in ourselves but in the One who is able to keep us true:

> To him who is able to keep you from falling and to present you before his glorious presence without fault and with great joy—to the only God our Savior be glory, majesty, power and authority, through Jesus Christ our Lord, before all ages, now and forevermore! Amen. (Jude 24–25)

NOTES

Acknowledgments
1. David M. Dawson Jr., *More Power to the Preacher* (Grand Rapids: Zondervan, 1956).

Introduction: A Noble Task
1. David Fisher, *The Twenty-First Century Pastor: A Vision Based on the Ministry of Paul* (Grand Rapids: Zondervan, 1996), 114.

Chapter 1: Your First Pastorate
1. Powhatan W. James, *George W. Truett: A Biography* (New York: Macmillan, 1945), 48–49; quoted in Clyde Fant and William Pinson, *Twenty Centuries of Great Preaching* (Waco: Word, 1971), 8:133–34.
2. Search committees are contrary to appropriate church polity in traditions that appoint ministers. They sometimes visit, nevertheless. If you are in such a tradition and a visit happens, be polite, but report the visit to your supervisor. When those in authority make a tentative assignment, you might be free to interview with a proper committee.
3. Jerry Falwell, *Falwell: An Autobiography* (Lynchburg, Va.: Liberty House, 1997), 212.
4. Benjamin Griffith, *A Short Treatise Concerning a True and Orderly Gospel Church* (Philadelphia: Philadelphia Baptist Assoc., 1743). Available online at www.founders.org./library/polity/griffith.

Chapter 2: The Pastor Among His People
1. William Croswell Doane, "The Preacher's Mistake," in *The Best Loved*

Poems of the American People, comp. Hazel Felleman (New York: Garden City Books, 1936), 339–40.
2. For more on this theme, see Austin B. Tucker, "Visiting in a New Age," *Church Administration* (October 1968): 40–41.
3. David M. Dawson Jr., *More Power to the Preacher* (Grand Rapids: Zondervan, 1956), 46.

Chapter 3: Pastoral Care and Counseling

1. John Drakeford, *The Awesome Power of the Listening Ear* (Waco: Word, 1967).
2. Lynn Vincent, "Breaking Faith," *World* 17, no. 12 (20 March 2002): 20.
3. Jay E. Adams, *Competent to Counsel: Introduction to Nouthetic Counseling* (Grand Rapids: Zondervan, 1970).
4. Three years later, Adams followed the great reception of this new approach to pastoral counseling with *The Christian Counselor's Manual* (Philadelphia: Presbyterian and Reformed, 1973). For a good critique of this approach to counseling, see J. D. Carter, "Nouthetic Counseling," in *Baker Encyclopedia of Psychology,* ed. David G. Benner (Grand Rapids: Baker, 1985).
5. Sam Stone, *The Christian Minister: A Practical Approach to the Preaching Ministry* (Cincinnati: Standard, 1991), 162.

Chapter 4: The Pastor's Pulpit Ministry

1. Bruce Corley, Steve Lemke, and Grant Lovejoy, eds., *Biblical Hermeneutics: A Comprehensive Introduction to Interpreting Scripture,* rev. ed. (Nashville: Broadman and Holman, 2002). For a good example of "historical-theological" hermeneutics, see Walter A. Elwell and Robert W. Yarbrough, *Encountering the New Testament: A Historical and Theological Survey* (Grand Rapids: Baker, 1998), 34, 153–67.
2. Karl Barth and Rudolf Bultmann both rejected special principles for interpreting Scripture. Bultmann said, "The interpretation of the Biblical Scriptures is not subject to any different conditions of understanding from any other literature." In *Church Dogmatics,* Karl Barth wrote, "There is no such thing as special biblical hermeneutics." Rudolf Bultmann, *Glaube and Verstehen II,* 231 and Karl Barth, *Die kirchliche Dogmatik* I/2, 515.
3. Andrew Blackwood, *The Preparation of Sermons* (New York: Abingdon-Cokesbury, 1948).
4. Halford E. Luccock, "Preaching to Life Situations," from *In the Minister's Workshop* (New York: Abingdon-Cokesbury, 1944), 52.
5. Rev. Lea tells this story on himself in Larry Lea, *Could You Not Tarry*

One Hour? (Lake Mary, Fla.: Creation House, 1987), 71. The foible was also claimed years earlier by humorist Bob Short, author of *The Gospel According to Peanuts* (1965; reprint, Louisville: Westminster John Knox, 2000), who, while a student pastor, once prayed in his Sunday evening pastoral prayer, "Forgive our falling shorts."

Chapter 5: Problem-Solving Preaching

1. C. H. Dodd, "Lecture I: The Primitive Preaching," in *The Apostolic Preaching and Its Development* (New York: Harper and Row, 1964), 7–35.
2. Philip Hacking, for one, takes issue with Fosdick's rule, saying, "The standard of a sermon is measured not by how many people stay to be counseled but by how few. Very often if the Word has been preached clearly it is a matter between the individual and the Lord." Hacking's judgment was that people stay for counseling because they are bewildered. "Some of the most effective meetings have been followed by a quiet going home to put right what God has clearly said to us." Philip Hacking, "Pastoral Preaching," in *A Passion for Preaching: Reflections on the Art of Preaching: Essays in Honor of Stephen F. Olford,* comp. David L. Olford (Nashville: Thomas Nelson, 1989), 107.
3. Fredrick W. Robertson, "The Loneliness of Christ," in *Treasury of the World's Great Sermons,* comp. Warren W. Wiersbe (Grand Rapids: Kregel, 1993), 495–99.
4. Harry Emerson Fosdick, *The Power to See It Through* (New York: Harper and Row, 1935), 1.
5. George W. Truett, "The Conquest of Fear," in *Follow Thou Me* (Nashville: Broadman, 1932), 103–14. Eight volumes of Truett's sermons are collected and reprinted in four paperback double volumes as the George W. Truett Library (Nashville: Broadman, 1980). Unfortunately, page numbers in the index to that set have no relationship to the actual pagination as printed.

Chapter 6: Pastoral Leadership

1. Leith Anderson is an example of one whose definition of leadership requires successful motivation of followers. He adapts the definition offered by John Mott, outstanding Christian statesman, Methodist layman, and successful founder and leader of the Christian Student Movement at the beginning of the twentieth century. In a chapter titled "Leaders Who Lead," Mott defined *leader* as "one who knows the road, who can keep ahead, and *who can pull others after him*" (emphasis added). Leith Anderson, *Dying for Change* (Minneapolis: Bethany House, 1990), 187.

2. George Barna, evangelical pollster, defines *leadership* as "the ability to motivate and lead institutional change." He is convinced that most pastors are not leaders. Barna's training in political science, especially polling, shapes his increasingly pessimistic view of the church. His model for church growth follows market theory requiring the leader to be a chief executive officer such as might run a large corporation. The shepherd and the flock seem far from his mind. His very popular books include *The Frog in the Kettle* (Ventura, Calif.: Regal, 1990); *User-Friendly Churches* (Ventura, Calif.: Regal, 1991); *The Power of Vision* (Ventura, Calif.: Regal, 1992); and *The Second Coming of the Church* (Ventura, Calif.: Regal, 1998). See also Tim Stafford, "The Third Coming of George Barna," *Christianity Today* (5 August 2002): 38.
3. Barna, *User-Friendly Churches*, 141–42.

Chapter 7: Conflict Management

1. The Sam Blizzard report in the 1960s surveyed thirteen hundred ministers. They were asked to rank six duties according to their importance. The most important duty was as a preacher, followed in order by pastor, priest, teacher, organizer, and administrator. When the same thirteen hundred pastors were asked to rank the same six duties according to the amount of time they actually spent in each task, the startling reversal was administrator first, then pastor, priest, organizer, preacher, and teacher. George Barna's research prints a similar profile of the pastor at the beginning of the twenty-first century. For example, when asked to identify their primary spiritual gift, 40 percent of senior pastors said preaching or teaching, 12 percent said pastoring, and only 4 percent said leadership. See Barna Research Online at www.barna.org [research archive: pastors], "Spiritual Gifts," 2001.
2. Thomas J. Peters and Robert H. Waterman Jr., *In Search of Excellence: Lessons from America's Best Run Companies* (New York: Harper and Row, 1982), 56–57. Pastors, in fact, do tend to rate themselves above average in nearly every category. In a 2001 survey by the Barna organization, nine of ten pastors gave themselves an "excellent" or a "good" rating on their preaching and teaching. Eighty-five percent did the same on their skill of encouraging people. More than eight of ten judged themselves excellent or good in the area of pastoring or shepherding people. Similar confidence marked their assessment of their own ability in other areas, such as motivating people, discipling or mentoring, evangelism, counseling, administration or management, and developing ministry strategy. The only tested element in which ministers judged themselves average or below was fund-raising, for

which only 31 percent claimed to be doing an above-average job. Of course, this element is more verifiable. But realistically, except at Lake Wobegon, no more than half of any group can be in the top half. See Barna Research Online at www.barna.org (research archive: pastors), "Getting the Job Done," 2001.
3. Leith Anderson, *Dying for Change* (Minneapolis: Bethany House, 1990), 191.

Chapter 8: Weddings and Funerals
1. See online www.covenantmarriage.com (research archive: covenant marriage), "Believing That Marriage Is a Covenant" and "What Are We Asking of Leaders?"

Chapter 9: Ministerial Ethics
1. Bruce Rosenstein, "Scandals Nothing New to Business Guru: A Conversation with Peter Drucker," *USA Today* (5 July 2002): 8B.
2. David M. Dawson Jr., *More Power to the Preacher* (Grand Rapids: Zondervan, 1956), 137–38.

Chapter 10: The Bivocational Pastor
1. Dennis W. Bickers, *The Tentmaking Pastor: The Joy of Bivocational Ministry* (Grand Rapids: Baker, 2000).
2. Compare Luther M. Dorr, *The Bivocational Pastor* (Nashville: Broadman, 1988), 35; and Gary E. Farley, "Consider Bivocationalism," *The Student* (August 1988): 1.
3. Henry Bettenson, ed., *Documents of the Christian Church* (London: Oxford University, 1944), 91–93.
4. Bickers, *The Tentmaking Pastor*.
5. Farley, "Consider Bivocationalism," 1–2. See also Bickers, *The Tentmaking Pastor;* and Dorr, *The Bivocational Pastor*.

Chapter 11: The Pastor as Teacher
1. Richard Baxter, *The Reformed Pastor* (1656; reprint, Portland, Ore.: Multnomah, 1982), 115.
2. Ibid., 79–80.

Chapter 12: The Pastor as Evangelist
1. Richard Ellsworth Day, *The Shadow of the Broad Brim: The Life Story of Charles Haddon Spurgeon, Heir of the Puritans* (Valley Forge, Pa.: Judson, 1934), 166.
2. Compare Robert Hall Glover, *The Progress of World-Wide Missions,* rev.

by J. Herbert Kane (New York: Harper and Brothers, 1960), 28–31. Glover and Kane note that early biographies of Mohammed "extol him as a virtuous man, a true patriot and a sincere philanthropist. Later ones swing to the opposite extreme and brand him as a monster of iniquity" (p. 29). Glover and Kane express their own conviction about the religion of Islam by endorsing a quote from Sir William Muir ending with the summary judgement: "The sword of Mohammed, and the Koran, are the most stubborn enemies of Civilization, Liberty, and Truth which the world has yet known" (pp. 30–31).
3. H. Grady Davis, *Design for Preaching* (Philadelphia: Muhlenberg, 1958), 139–62. One of the more recent textbooks following this plan is Haddon W. Robinson, *Biblical Preaching: The Development and Delivery of Expository Sermons* (Grand Rapids: Baker, 1980), 115–25.
4. See Gideon G. Yoder, "The Religion of Childhood and Adolescence," in *The Nurture and Evangelism of Children* (Scottsdale, Pa.: Herald, 1954), 73–109.
5. Gaines Dobbins, *A Ministering Church* (Nashville: Broadman, 1960), 191. Admittedly, Dobbins wrote before the day of modern telemarketing. Today, great resistance exists to strangers canvassing by telephone, but, if it were not profitable for the telemarketers, they would give it up. It can be done with a personal touch, and, no doubt, many lonely people are glad to know that someone cares about them.

Chapter 13: Baptism and the Lord's Supper
1. John R. W. Stott, "Charles Simeon: A Personal Appreciation," introduction to Charles Simeon, *Evangelical Preaching* (Portland, Ore.: Multnomah, 1986), xxviii–xxix.
2. Charles L. Rice, *The Embodied Word: Preaching as Art and Liturgy* (Minneapolis: Augsburg Fortress, 1991), 57.

Chapter 14: The Pastor's Stewardship of Time
1. Rick Warren, *The Purpose-Driven Life: What on Earth Am I Here For?* (Grand Rapids: Zondervan, 2002), 22. Warren summarizes God's purposes for creating humankind as: ". . . for God's pleasure, . . . for God's family, . . . to become like Christ, . . . for serving God and . . . for a mission."
2. Julie Morgenstern, *Time Management from the Inside Out: The Foolproof System for Taking Control of Your Schedule and Your Life* (New York: Henry Holt, 2000), 63.
3. Rosalind Rinker, *Prayer, Conversing with God* (Grand Rapids: Zondervan, 1959).
4. In the fall, you will probably need extra time for planning next year's

calendar. Some of this time will probably be evening meetings because you will want to involve lay leaders in the planning.
5. Some churches prefer to make the major outreach emphasis on Friday or Saturday or both. It is closer to the coming Sunday, but having it early in the week has the advantage of being closer to the Sunday that just passed, when you usually receive the names of those who need your visit.
6. Jean-Louis Servan-Schreiber, *The Art of Time*, trans. Eva and Leo Sartori, based on a previous translation by Franklin Philip (New York: Marlowe, 1988, 2000), 138–39.
7. Austin B. Tucker, "Monroe Elmon Dodd and His Preaching" (Th.D. dissertation, Southwestern Baptist Theological Seminary, Fort Worth, Texas, July 1971). See also Stephen Nelson Rummage, *Planning Your Preaching: A Step-by-Step Guide for Developing a One-Year Preaching Calendar* (Grand Rapids: Kregel, 2002).
8. Consider the plural form *elders* in Acts 14:23; 20:17; Philippians 1:1; 1 Timothy 5:17; and Titus 1:5. The term *elder* has a long history in the Hebrew Bible and in the New Testament, where the Sanhedrin is a "Council of Elders." As for the *angels* of the seven churches in Revelation, the word translated *angel* means "messenger," whether heavenly or earthly. It might refer to the pastor. But admitting that it does, note that the ministers are also called *a star* collectively, so the singular *angel* might refer to the messengers collectively or to one senior pastor. It is not clear in history when churches began to have only one pastor, but it does seem clear that the New Testament pattern was a plurality of elders.

Chapter 15: The Pastor's Personal Life

1. *Investor's Business Daily*, 6 September 2002, A2.
2. At this writing, tax advantages are available to pastors and others who receive a housing allowance or have a house provided by their employer. A case pending in the U.S. federal courts was sparked unwittingly by Rick Warren, pastor of Saddleback Community Church. An activist court agreed with his case against the IRS setting arbitrary "fair market value" on his house. Then they used that occasion to visit the uncontested issue of whether the "housing allowance" exemption is at all constitutional. Congress rushed through a law with almost unanimous bipartisan support, affirming the exemption. Nevertheless, at this writing, it remains to be seen what the courts will say about the constitutional issue.
3. Ralph G. Turnbull, *A Minister's Obstacles* (New York: Revell, 1946), 23.

SELECT BIBLIOGRAPHY

THIS READING LIST, LIKE THE WHOLE BOOK, seeks to meet the need of the beginning pastor or ministerial student. It includes a number of titles that are not cited in the preceding pages, and some of the works cited earlier are not included here. Instead, it is a collection of titles that are likely to be helpful to you, the reader, as you begin your pilgrimage of pastoral ministry.

Because the pastor is a minister of the Word above all else, the first grouping includes books that will help you nourish your own soul, inform your labor, and equip you to teach and preach to others.

Tools for Bible Study

Aland, Barbara, Kurt Alund, Johannes Karavidopoulos, Carlo M. Martini, and Bruce M. Metzger, eds. *The Greek New Testament*. 4th rev. ed. New York: United Bible Societies, 1983.

Arnold, Bill T., and Bryan E. Beyer, *Encountering the Old Testament: A Christian Survey*. Grand Rapids: Baker, 1999. Interactive CD-ROM study aid included.

Beitzel, Barry, ed. *The Moody Atlas of Bible Lands*. Chicago: Moody, 1985.

Corley, Bruce, Steve Lemke, and Grant Lovejoy, eds. *Biblical Hermeneutics: A Comprehensive Introduction to Interpreting Scripture*. Rev. ed. Nashville: Broadman and Holman, 2002.

Elwell, Walter A., ed. *Baker Encyclopedia of the Bible.* 4 vols. Grand Rapids: Baker, 1997.
Elwell, Walter A., and Robert W. Yarbrough. *Encountering the New Testament: A Historical and Theological Survey.* Grand Rapids: Baker, 1998. Interactive CD-ROM study aid included.
Fee, Gordon D., and Douglas Stuart. *How to Read the Bible for All Its Worth: A Guide to Understanding the Bible.* Grand Rapids: Zondervan, 1982.
Goodrick, Edward W., and John R. Kohlenberger III. *The NIV Exhaustive Concordance.* Grand Rapids: Zondervan, 1990.
Kohlenberger, John R., III. *The Precise Parallel New Testament: Greek Text, King James Version, Rheimes Bible, New International Version, New Revised Standard Version, New American Bible, Amplified Bible.* New York: Oxford, 1995.
Wallace, Daniel B. *The Basics of New Testament Syntax: An Intermediate Greek Grammar, the Abridgement of Greek Grammar Beyond the Basics.* Grand Rapids: Zondervan, 2000.

Preaching and Teaching

Brooks, Phillips. *Lectures on Preaching.* New York: E. P. Dutton and Co., 1877.
Craddock, Fred B. *Preaching.* Nashville: Abingdon, 1985.
Davis, H. Grady. *Design for Preaching.* Philadelphia: Muhlenberg, 1958.
Hughes, Robert G. *A Trumpet in Darkness: Preaching to Mourners.* Philadelphia: Fortress, 1985.
Jowett, John H. *The Preacher: His Life and Work.* New York: Harper and Bros., 1912.
Lenski, R. C. H. *The Sermon: Its Homiletical Construction.* 1912. Reprint, Grand Rapids: Baker, 1968.
McDill, Wayne. *The Twelve Essential Skills for Great Preaching.* Nashville: Broadman and Holman, 1994.
Robinson, Haddon W. *Biblical Preaching: The Development and Delivery of Expository Messages.* Grand Rapids: Baker, 2001.
Rummage, Stephen Nelson. *Planning Your Preaching: A Step-by-Step Guide for Developing a One-Year Preaching Calendar.* Grand Rapids: Kregel, 2002.
Stott, John R. W. *Between Two Worlds: The Art of Preaching in the Twentieth Century.* Grand Rapids: Eerdmans, 1982.

Pastoral Care and Counseling

Adams, Jay. *The Christian Counselor's Manual.* Philadelphia: Presbyterian and Reformed, 1973.

Benner, David G., ed. *Baker Encyclopedia of Psychology*. Grand Rapids: Baker, 1985.
Jefferson, Charles. *The Minister as Shepherd*. 1946, reprint. Fincastle, Va.: Scripture Truth, n.d.
Oates, Wayne E. *The Christian Pastor*. Philadelphia: Westminster, 1951.
Platt, Larry A., and Roger G. Branch. *Resources for Ministry in Death and Dying*. Nashville: Broadman, 1988.

Pastoral Administration and Ministry

Anderson, Leith. *Dying for Change*. Minneapolis: Bethany House, 1990.
Barna, George. *User-Friendly Churches: What Christians Need to Know About the Churches People Love to Go To*. Ventura, Calif.: Regal, 1999.
Baxter, Richard. *The Reformed Pastor*. Based on William Orme's 1830 edition. Portland, Ore.: Multnomah, 1982.
Bickers, Dennis W. *The Tentmaking Pastor: The Joy of Bivocational Ministry*. Grand Rapids: Baker, 2000.
Cothen, Joe H. *Equipped for Good Work*. Gretna, La.: Pelican, 1981.
Dale, Robert D. *Pastoral Leadership*. Nashville: Broadman, 1960.
Dawson, David M., Jr. *More Power to the Preacher*. Grand Rapids: Zondervan, 1956.
Fisher, David. *The Twenty-first Century Pastor: A Vision Based on the Ministry of Paul*. Grand Rapids: Zondervan, 1966.
Goodykoontz, Henry G. *The Minister in the Reformed Tradition*. Richmond: John Knox, 1963.
Hobbs, J. R. *The Pastor's Manual*. Nashville: Broadman, 1934.
Riley, W. B. *Pastoral Problems*. Westwood, N.J.: Revell, 1959.
Tillapaugh, Frank R. *The Church Unleashed*. Ventura, Calif.: Regal, 1982.
Turnbull, Ralph G. *A Minister's Obstacles*. Westwood, N.J.: Revell, 1946.

Evangelism and Missions

Coleman, Robert E. *The Master Plan of Evangelism*. Westwood, N.J.: Revell, 1964.
Evans, William, *Personal Soul-Winning*. Chicago: Moody, 1910.
Glover, Robert Hall, and J. Herbert Kane. *The Progress of World-Wide Missions*. New York: Harper and Bros., 1960.
Miles, Delos. *Introduction to Evangelism*. Nashville: Broadman, 1983.
Sweazey, George E. *Effective Evangelism*. Grand Rapids: Eerdmans, 1976.

To receive a sample form for indexing pastoral illustrations developed by the author, write to Austin B. Tucker, c/o Kregel Publications, Inc., P.O. Box 2607, Grand Rapids, MI 49501-2607 or e-mail: abtucker@kregel.com.